A V█████████████Plays

'Set at the point where reality and ideology rub up against each other, Franca Rame and Dario Fo's monologues are vivid, concise and entertaining comments on the female condition . . . comic-but-angry, raw-but-precise.'
                                        Alex Renton, *Independent*

The twenty monologues for women in this volume range from the deadly serious to the extravagantly comic, using comedy as a weapon that makes sexual politics accessible to a wide range of audiences.

Edited by Stuart Hood and translated by Gillian Hanna, who performed a selection of pieces to great critical acclaim at the Half Moon Theatre, London in 1989; Ed Emery, political activist and translator of Fo's *Mistero Buffo*; and Christopher Cairns, Italianist and Lecturer in Italian Drama at the University College of Wales in Aberystwyth.

FRANCA RAME and DARIO FO were highly successful in writing, directing and performing satirical comedies for the conventional theatre in the Fifties. In the Sixties they abandoned it. Fo began to write for a wider audience in factories and workers' clubs and produced work which was not only an important political contribution in Italy but has been internationally acclaimed. In 1970 Fo and Rame founded the theatrical collective, La Comune, in Milan. Fo's work – and the work of Franca Rame – has been performed in Britain with great success: *Can't Pay? Won't Pay!* (Half Moon Theatre and Criterion Theatre, London, 1981); *Accidental Death of an Anarchist* (Half Moon Theatre and Wyndham's Theatre, London, 1980); *Female Parts* by Franca Rame (National Theatre, London, 1981); *Mistero Buffo* (Riverside Theatre, London, 1983); *Trumpets and Raspberries* (Palace Theatre, Watford; Phoenix Theatre, London, 1984); *Archangels Don't Play Pinball* (Bristol Old Vic, 1986); *Elizabeth* (Half Moon Theatre, London, 1986), *An Ordinary Day* (Borderline Theatre Company, Scotland, touring, 1988) and *The Pope and the Witch* (West Yorkshire Playhouse, Leeds, 1991; Comedy Theatre, London, 1992). In 1997 Dario Fo was awarded the Nobel Prize for Literature.

FRANCA RAME
and
DARIO FO

A Woman Alone & Other Plays

translated by GILLIAN HANNA, ED EMERY
and CHRISTOPHER CAIRNS

Introduced by STUART HOOD
and GILLIAN HANNA

Methuen Drama

METHUEN DRAMA MODERN PLAYS

13 15 14

First published in these translations in Great Britain in 1991 by
Methuen Publishing Limited

Methuen Drama
A&C Black Publishers Ltd
38 Soho Square, London W1D 3HB

A Woman Alone, Rise and Shine, Bless Me Father For I Have Sinned,
The Same Old Story, Medea, The Rape, Alice in Wonderless Land, The
Whore in the Madhouse, Coming Home, I'm Ulrike-Screaming, It
Happened Tomorrow translation copyright © Gillian Hanna
MicheleLu Lanzone, Nada Pasini Fascism 1922, An Arab Woman
Speaks, The Eel-Woman, Mamma Togni, The Bawd – The Christian
Democrat Party in Chile, The Mother translation copyright © 1991
Ed Emery
The Dancing Mistress: On the Assembly Line translation copyright ©
1991 Christopher Cairns
Introduction copyright © 1991 Gillian Hanna
General Introduction © 1991 Methuen Drama
The authors have asserted their moral rights

A CIP Catalogue record for this book is available from the British
Library

ISBN 978-0-413-64030-7

The front cover shows Gillian Hanna in *A Common Woman*, a selection
of one-woman plays by Franca Rame and Dario Fo
Photo by Gerry Murray

Printed and bound in Great Britain by
Biddles Ltd., King's Lynn, Norfolk
Photoset by Rowland Phototypesetting Ltd,
Bury St Edmunds, Suffolk

Contents

INTRODUCTION
The Theatre of Dario Fo and Franca Rame

The son of a railway worker, Dario Fo was born in 1926 near the Lago Maggiore in Northern Italy. He grew up in a village community that included glass-blowers and smugglers, where there was a strong tradition of popular narrative – much of it humourously subversive of authority – fed by travelling story-tellers and puppeteers. Gifted artistically, he studied architecture at Milan at the art-school attached to the Brera Gallery; but the theatre drew him strongly – first as a set-designer and then as a performer. His career began in revue which was the spectacular escapist entertainment of post-war Italy with girls and comics (some very brilliant like Totò, whom Fo greatly admired) and glamorous *chanteuses*. It was a genre favoured by politicians of the ruling Christian Democrat party; girls' legs were preferable to the social preoccupations of contemporary Italian cinema. In revue Fo began to make his mark as an extraordinarily original comic and mime. On radio he built a reputation with his monologues as a Poer Nano – the poor simpleton who, in telling Bible stories, for example, gets things wrong, preferring Cain to the insufferable prig, Abel. In 1954 he married Franca Rame, a striking and talented actress, who came from a family of travelling players and had made her first stage appearance when she was eight days old. Together they embarked on a highly successful series of productions.

In the fifties the right-wing clerical Christian Democrat government had imposed a tight censorship on film, theatre and broadcasting. Fo took advantage of a slght relaxation in censorship to mount an 'anti-revue', *Il dito nell'occhio* (One in the Eye). His aim was clear – to attack those myths in Italian life which, as he said, 'Fascism had imposed and Christian Democracy had preserved.' *Il dito nell'occhio* was 'one in the eye' for official versions of history. Presented at the Piccolo Teatro in Milan it was an immense success to which the participation of the great French mime, Jacques Lecoq, from whom Fo learned much, was an important contribution. *Il dito nell'occhio* was the first in a series of pieces which drew on French farce, on the traditional sketches of the Rame family, and on the traditions of the circus. This mixture of spectacle, mime and social comment was highly successful but made the authorities nervous; the police were frequently present at performances, following the scripts with pocket torches to ensure that there were no departures from the officially approved text. Fo grew in stature and virtuosity as actor and comic, exploiting his extraordinary range of gesture, movement and facial expression, his variety of voices and accents, and his skill as a story-teller. It was the misfortune of Italian cinema that it was unable to exploit his talents. There were difficulties in finding suitable scripts and, on set, his vitality and spontaneity were denied the space and freedom that the theatre provided. But what Fo did take away from film was an understanding of how montage gave pace to narrative.

In 1959 the Dario Fo–Franca Rame company was invited to open a season at the Odeon Theatre in Milan. The piece they chose was *Gli arcangeli non giocano a flipper* (Archangels Don't Play Pinball), written, directed and designed by Fo. It was unusual in that it dealt critically with certain ludicrous aspects of Italian society. The middle-class audience were astonished by its rhythms and technique and delighted by Fo in the leading role – that of a wise simpleton, who looks back to Poer Nano and forward to a series of similar clowns in later work. Fo and Rame were now securely established both as actors and as personalities in the public eye. Their success in conventional theatre was confirmed by a series of pieces which exploited a mixture of comedy, music and farcical plots in which Fo would, for instance, double as an absent-minded priest and a bandit. The social references were there – Fo and Rame were now both close to the Communist Party and acutely aware of the political tensions in society – and the public readily picked them up. In a period which saw widespread industrial unrest culminating in the general strike of 1960 their material caused the authorities in Milan to threaten to ban performances.

Italian television had been for many years a fief of the Christian Democrats. Programme control was strict: a young woman given to wearing tight sweaters who looked like winning a popular quiz show had to be eliminated on moral grounds. But when in 1962 the centre-left of the Christian Democrats became dominant there was some relaxation of censorship. It was in these circumstances that the Fo–Rame team was invited to appear on the most popular TV show, *Canzonissima*, which, as its name suggests, featured heart-throb singers along with variety acts. Into this show the Fo's proceeded to inject their own variety of subversive humour – such as a sketch in which a worker whose aunt has fallen into a mincing-machine, which cannot be stopped for that would interrupt production, piously takes her home as tinned meat. The reaction of the political authorities and of the right-wing press was to call for censorship, duly imposed by the obedient functionaries of Italian television – all of them political appointees. There was a tussle of wills at the end of which the Fo's walked out of the show. The scandal was immense. There were parliamentary questions; threats of law-suits on both sides. Fo had public opinion solidly behind him. He had, he said, tried to look behind the facade of the 'economic miracle', to question the view that 'we were all one big family now' and to show how exploitation had increased and scandals flourished. By subverting *Canzonissima* from within he had established himself with a huge popular audience.

During this period Fo had become interested in material set in or drawn from the Middle Ages. He had begun 'to look at the present with the instruments of history and culture in order to judge it better'. He invited the public to use these instruments by writing an ambiguous piece, *Isabella, tre caravelle e un cacciaballe* (Isabella, Three Caravels and a Wild-Goose Chaser), in which Columbus – that schoolbook hero – is portrayed as the upwards striving intellectual who loses out in the game of high politics. It was a period when Brecht's *Galileo* was playing with great success in Milan and the theatre was a subject of intense debate in the intellectual and political ferment leading up to the unrest of 1968. For Fo the most important result was probably his collaboration with a group of left-wing musicians who had become interested in the political potential of popular songs. Their work appealed to him because he was himself 'interested above all in a past attached to the roots of the people .   . and the concept of "the new in

the traditional"'.' They put together a show, built round
popular and radical songs, to which Fo contributed his theories
on the importance of gesture and the rhythms in the
performances of folksong; it marked an important step in his
development.

In 1967 he put on his last production for the bourgeois
theatre, *La signora non è da buttare* (The Lady's Not For
Discarding), in which a circus was made the vehicle for an
attack on the United States and capitalist society in general. It
again attracted the attention of the authorities. Fo was called
to police headquarters in Milan and threatened with arrest for
'offensive lines', not included in the approved version,
attacking a head of state – Lyndon Johnson. By now it was
becoming 'more and more difficult to act in a theatre where
everything down to the subdivision of the seating . . . mirrored
the class divisions. The choice for an intellectual', Fo
concluded, 'was to leave his gilded ghetto and put himself at
the disposal of the movement.'

The company with which the Fo's confronted this task was
the cooperative Nuova Scena – an attempt to dispense with the
traditional roles in a stage company and to make decision-
making collective. It was, Fo said in retrospect, a utopian
project in which individual talents and capabilities were
sacrificed to egalitarian principles. But whatever the internal
difficulties there was no doubt as to the success the company
enjoyed with a new public which it sought out in the working-
class estates, in cooperatives and trade union halls, in factories
and workers' clubs. It was a public which knew nothing of the
theatre but which found the political attitudes the company
presented close to its experience of life. Each performance was
followed by a discussion.

Nuova Scena did not last long – it was torn apart by political
arguments, by arguments over the relationship of art to society
and politics, and by questions of organisation. There were also
difficulties with the Communist Party, which often controlled
the premises used and whose officials began to react negatively
to satirical attacks on their bureaucracy, the inflexibility of the
Party line, the intolerance of real discussion. Before the split
came, the company had put on a *Grande pantomima con
bandiere e pupazzi medi e piccoli* (Grand Pantomime with

Flags and Little and Medium Puppets), in which Fo used a huge puppet, drawn from the Sicilian tradition, to represent the state and its continual fight with the 'dragon' of the working class. But the most important production was Fo's one-man show *Mistero Buffo*, which was to become one of his enduring triumphs in Italy and abroad. In it he drew on the counter-culture of the Middle Ages, on apocryphal gospel stories, on legend and tales, presenting episodes in which he played all the roles and used a language in part invented, in part archaic, in part drawn from the dialects of Northern Italy. It has been described as 'an imaginary Esperanto of the poor and the disinherited'. In performing the scenes of which *Mistero Buffo* is composed – such as the resurrection of Lazarus, the marriage at Cana, Pope Boniface's encounter with Jesus on the Via Dolorosa and others – Fo drew on two main traditions: that of the *giullare* (inadequately translated into English as 'jester'), the travelling comic, singer, mime, who in the Middle Ages was the carrier of a subversive culture; and that of the great clowns of the Commedia dell'Arte with their use of masks, of dialect and of *grammelot*, that extraordinary onomatopoeic rendering of a language – French, say – invented by the 15th-century comedians in which there are accurate sounds and intonations but few real words, all adding up (with the aid of highly expressive mime) to intelligible discourse.

When Nuova Scena split in 1970 it came hard on the heels of mounting polemics in the Communist press. Looking back, Franca Rame has admitted that she and Dario Fo were perhaps sectarian and sometimes mistaken but that they had had to break with the Communist cultural organisations if they wished to progress. The result was La Comune, a theatre company with its headquarters in Milan. The Fo's were now politically linked to the new Left, which found the Communist Party too authoritarian, too locked in the mythology of the Resistance, too inflexible and increasingly conservative. In *Morte accidentale di un'anarchico* (Accidental Death of an Anarchist) Fo produced a piece in which his skill at writing farce and his gifts as a clown were put brilliantly at the service of his politics, playing on the tension between the real death of a prisoner and the farcical inventions advanced by the authorities to explain it.

It is estimated that in four years the piece was seen by a million people, many of whom took part in fierce debates after the performance. Fo had succeeded in his aim of making of the theatre 'a great machine which makes people laugh at dramatic things . In the laughter there remains a sediment of anger.' So no easy catharsis. There followed a period in which Fo was deeply engaged politically – both through his writings and through his involvement with Franca Rame, who was the main mover of the project – in Red Aid, which collected funds and comforts for Italian political prisoners detained in harsh conditions. His writing dealt with the Palestinian struggle, with Chile, with the methods of the Italian police. In the spring of 1973 Franca Rame was kidnapped from her home in Milan by a Fascist gang, gravely assaulted and left bleeding in the street. Fo himself later that year was arrested and held in prison in Sardinia for refusing to allow police to be present at rehearsals. Demonstrations and protests ensured his release. Dario Fo had, as his lawyer said, for years no longer been only an actor but a political figure whom the state powers would use any weapon to silence.

His political flair was evident in the farce *Non si paga, non si paga* (Can't Pay? Won't Pay!) dating from 1974, which deals with the question of civil disobedience. Significantly, the main upholder of law and order is a Communist shop steward, who disapproves of his wife's gesture of rebellion against the rising cost of living – a raid on a supermarket. It was a piece tried out on and altered at the suggestion of popular audiences – a practice Fo has often used. It was the same spirit that inspired his *Storia di una tigre* (Story of a Tiger), an allegorical monologue dating from 1980 – after a trip to China, and based on a Chinese folktale – the moral of which is that, if you have 'tiger' in you, you must never delegate responsibility to others, never expect others to solve your own problems, and above all avoid that unthinking party loyalty which is the enemy of reason and of revolution. In 1981, following on the kidnapping of Aldo Moro came *Clacson, trombette e pernacchi* (Trumpets and Raspberries). In it Fo doubled as Agnelli, the boss of FIAT, and a FIAT shop steward, whose identities become farcically confused. The play mocks the police and their readiness to see terrorists everywhere and the political cynicism which led to Moro's being abandoned to his fate by his fellow-politicians.

It was the last of Fo's major political works in a period when the great political upsurges in Western Europe have died away and consumerism has apparently triumphed. Yet even when he turned to a play about Elizabeth and Essex, *Almost by Chance a Woman: Elizabeth* with a splendid transvestite part for himself as a bawd, it was possible to read in his portrayal of the machinations of Cecil, Elizabeth's spymaster, a reference to the part played by secret services in Italian politics in the Seventies – and, it might be added, in other Western states. In the meantime he has produced for a theatrical festival in Venice a charming Harlequinade, which is an exercise in the techniques of the Commedia dell'Arte, the tradition from which he has drawn much of his inspiration. His latest play, *The Pope and the Witch*, is once more political not merely in its anti-clericalism – his return to Italian television at the end of the Eighties deeply upset the Catholic hierarchy – but in that it deals with the social problem of drugs and the debate as to whether the solution is to be found in police action or in more enlightened policies which address the needs of the addicts and the social conditions that lead to addiction. It is a piece which has found a strong resonance with Italian audiences.

Meanwhile Franca Rame, who has progressively established herself as a political figure and a powerful feminist voice, has produced performances of a number of one-woman plays in collaboration with her husband – monologues usually which are a direct political intervention in a society where the role of women is notably restricted by the Church, the state and male traditions. Like her husband she finds political intervention difficult in a period which she defines as being one of indifference, of cynicism, of alienation – one in which the grand social causes have been replaced by other issues, green issues, issues affecting deprived children, children with congenital defects, issues like those of drugs and AIDS which are indeed political and of almost universal application.

To find a parallel to the role of Franca Rame and Dario Fo in the Italian theatre we have to go back to the second half of the 16th century when one of the most famous companies of the

Commedia dell'Arte was led by a husband and wife: Isabella and Francesco Andreini.

Franca Rame and Dario Fo came to the theatre by different routes. She comes from a family of travelling players and made her first appearance on stage as a babe-in-arms; Dario Fo came to the theatre through stage-design. Both had highly successful careers in conventional, bourgeois theatre which they abandoned in the Sixties to find new, popular audiences in unorthodox settings: circus tents, parking lots, piazzas. Their kind of theatre was a political intervention which reflected the radical movements on the Left in Italy in the Sixties and Seventies. The sharp, satirical nature of their work brought them into difficulties with the State, and with the Italian Communist Party, which was too inflexible to cope with the new forces in politics – young people, women and workers rebelling against the old industrial and political structures. They were inevitably attacked – in Franca Rame's case physically – by the neo-Fascists.

Their dramatic strategy was to use laughter as a weapon directed against conformism, against the duplicity of the government which deliberately created an atmosphere of tension; they were on the side of the oppressed – in particular of women. Like others who were politically active in those days they have had to rethink their strategies and targets. Their latest pieces – *The Pope and the Witch* and *Hush, We're Falling Head over Heels* – deal with the problems of drugs and AIDS. But their kind of theatre still draws on the great comic traditions of the Commedia dell'Arte, which they have kept alive and developed to deal with the social problems of today.

STUART HOOD
January 1991

INTRODUCTION
Performing in the Mirror

'The function of our theatre is to try to provoke self-awareness in the audience, a consciousness of what's going on around them, and to provide, in a sense, a mirror of society,' said Franca Rame in an interview on BBC's *Woman's Hour*.* At a time of so-called 'post-feminism', these plays are a bracing antidote to the wishful thinking that would consign the struggles of the last twenty years to the safe obscurity of history. As Rame says, 'I draw on problems that women have within the family, problems that women have at work, in the factories, in the office, and, of course, problems that they have within society at large.' That these problems have not been resolved is what gives her work its continuing painful resonance. Rame continues, 'The most important thing, the crucial thing that I would wish to see, that I would demand, is respect for women everywhere: at home, in the street, in the family and in bed. (*She laughs*) Very important.'

Here is what makes Rame's voice so special and unexpected. She is passionate in pursuit of change in society's attitudes to women. For her, it is not only a question of equal rights or equal pay at work. She also, critically, recognises the essential human flashpoint: emotional and sexual relationships between men and women, the enchantment and traps of heterosexual love. In the play *Coming Home* the wife's most bitter complaint against her husband is that he doesn't satisfy her sexually. Rame constantly challenges us to acknowledge that for women to achieve true equality the world has to be remade, in bed as much as at work.

None of the issues she tackles in these plays is new. After more than twenty years of the 'second wave' of feminism, her audience will be familiar with the themes. But they are issues that do not go away, and many are not amenable to legislative

---

* Franca Rame, Interview with Jill Burridge, *Woman's Hour*, BBC Radio 4, January 1991.

solutions. As long as men continue to abandon their middle-aged wives for 'younger flesh, younger skin', as long as women live in fear of rape, as long as women have to do two jobs – one inside, one outside the home – as long as women are forbidden to explore and enjoy their sexuality in a society that labels them as whores, so long will Rame's women continue to sing out loudly, so long will her audience recognise their voices.

The essential problem for both translator and performer is the question of finding this voice. When Franca Rame performs the plays in Italy she is already well known in her own right. Her audience is aware of her history as a political being as well as an actress. She appears on the stage bringing with her the ghost of three decades of political activity, and everyone in the audience, be it in a theatre or sports stadium or factory is familiar with that. So whichever character she is playing, her audience recognises her within all her characters. This is not to imply a lack of technical skill, to say that the actress somehow does not get inside the character she is playing. Quite the reverse, her virtuosity enables her to move seamlessly between herself and her characters. It enables her to speak to the audience through her characters. But her history means that she can also speak directly to the audience with authority and without the mediating force of those characters. When she performs these plays, she starts the evening as herself. She challenges the audience head on saying, in so many words: look, you know who I am, I want you to think about the shitty way women get treated in this world and this is how I am going to make you deal with it.

Rame is quoted as having said that she would like these plays to become part of an actress's repertoire. They are indeed, performed over and over again. But for any other performer and for the translator there are problems to be overcome. It has always seemed to me to be of vital importance to find the voice of each character, because it is almost impossible for any other actress to have the same direct (unspoken) line of communication to the audience that Rame does in the course of a performance. When that essential link is absent some other way has to be found of confronting the audience face to face with the urgency of what Rame, the writer, is saying.

The first question to be addressed always has to be: how can this be translated so that it can be *performed* effectively? Or, at its most basic, what works? Theatre is a collaborative art, and translations of plays, unlike other literary works, have to take *three* participants into account: author, performer and audience.

'What works?' has to be asked of these plays in the context of what Rame sets out to accomplish both politically and theatrically. They are passionate, angry, moving, and, in some cases, hilarious demands for a reappraisal of women's role in society. It is the job of the translator and the performer to move the audience through anger or tears or laughter to *rethink* the issues that Rame is throwing in their face.

This point is particularly tricky when dealing with the comic plays, and leads to a crucial issue: whether to leave the character in an Italian context or to move her to a place which the audience is likely to recognise more immediately, and where there is a greater chance of them laughing *with* the character rather than *at* her. The response Rame is looking for is not 'O look at this woman, isn't she funny?', but 'O God, that's hysterical, I've been there, I've done that ' The humour is the shared humour of what is common to all women. Additionally, it is a problem for the performer. If the character remains in her Italian surroundings, how is one to perform that? In English with an Italian accent? Not a good idea, given the unfortunate English tendency to find any foreigner funny just by dint of being foreign. Estelle Parsons, who is closely associated with Rame's work in America, leaves the plays in their original context and performs them as Italian-American women. This may be a solution in the United States where there is a large community of Italian descent which plays a vocal and visible role in mainstream American life, but would not be particularly helpful to performers in the British Isles (except, perhaps in Scotland, where there is also a lively Italian community). There is a danger, too, that by leaving the women in an Italian context they become generalised, their 'Italianness' having the effect of masking the differences between them – differences of age, class, temperament and attitude. As a performer my instinct has led me, in translating the plays, to look for the distance between the characters. I have tried to place them in such a way that each one's individual voice can be heard. The aim is to retain Franca Rame's savage bite, her precise wit and her passion, without depending on the actual presence of Rame herself.

Any actress who performs these plays quickly experiences the power of the relationship that is created between herself and the audience. This is indeed precisely why they are entering the repertoire of many actresses, as Rame had hoped. The plays demand that the performer redefine the relationship with the audience: the breaking down of the traditional fourth wall so that each character can speak *directly* to the audience.

Most of the plays require the performer to treat the audience as a trusted friend, a confidante. The context in which the plays function is often a domestic one and the performer has to establish the feeling of a woman leaning over the garden fence chatting to a neighbour. This is most obvious in *A Woman Alone*, where the character is actually talking to the audience-as-neighbour, but even in those plays which have a less domestic situation (*The Rape* and *Medea* for example) the performer has to buttonhole the audience by taking the characters out of the epic and into the intimate. In the end, Rame brings us back to the old adage of the Women's Movement: the personal is the political. Each member of the audience leaves the theatre knowing that the performer has been speaking to them individually.

My thanks are due to Sharon Miller, who directed the three pieces which made up *A Common Woman* (*Bless Me Father For I Have Sinned*, *The Rape*, *Coming Home*), and whose continued comments and suggestions have been an invaluable help. Thanks, too, to Diane Gelon for her expert skills in the preparation of the text.

GILLIAN HANNA
February 1991

All Home Bed and Church

A Woman Alone (1977)
Rise and Shine (1977)
Bless Me Father For I Have Sinned (1977)
The Same Old Story (1977)
Medea (1977)

The monologues in this volume are almost all pieces written – as Dario Fo says – as 'duets' by Franca Rame and himself. Often she would suggest an idea, he would make a treatment and then write the script. Sometimes she would propose an outline, he gave his views of it, and she finished the text. But usually the final working-out of the texts took place on-stage, taking into account the reaction of the audience – 'always our best collaborators'.

The monologues date in part from the late Sixties and Seventies – a period of intense political activity, of radicalism and terrorism and repression. To discredit the Left the government encouraged a policy of tension and used supergrasses to break the armed terrorist groups like the Red Brigade. It was also a period when the Italian women's movement asserted itself in campaigns for the right to legal abortion, to divorce and for equal rights at home and at work.

The group of monologues was first performed by Franca Rame in Milan in 1977. Subsequently she performed it all over Italy for women's groups, the box-office takings being used for the needs of the movement, for factory occupations, for setting up counselling centres. She was to give more than three thousand performances in Italy, in other European countries and in the Americas.

The first piece, *A Woman Alone*, she describes as being about a housewife or rather *the* housewife who has everything in the bosom of her family except the most important thing: the right to be treated by the men of the house as an individual, and respected as such, not used only as a sexual object and an unsalaried servant.

In *Rise and Shine*, she has written, 'we have a woman, a worker, doubly exploited, at home as a skivvy and in the factory. This is a figure – it is well to remember – who plays an important role in our society; it was absolutely necessary to speak of her'.

'There is nothing to be said about *Bless Me Father For I Have Sinned*,' she says, 'except to advise all women in the audience to ponder on the choice of ways of life open to this punk mother.'

'*The Same Old Story* presents a sexual relationship between a man and a woman . . . It is a fairy-tale which in its structure copies the old Sicilian stories with all the classical ingredients: the wolf, the witch and a few other characters: the good girl, the rag doll who uses bad language, the wicked red cat who stands for the male partner who should always be a comrade – above all at home – not only outside.

'*Medea* by Euripides is in a comic-grotesque key. We chose it on purpose because, first of all, we women have been weeping for two thousand years and this time we laugh and perhaps laugh over it afterwards because as a gentleman who understood about the theatre, a certain Molière, said: "Laughter makes you open your mouth wide – and your brain as well – and the nails of reason pierce your brain" '

STUART HOOD

When Franca Rame performs *Medea*, she does it in an idiom, a dialect that produces a woman rooted in the earth, in reality. I have tried to render this in simple plain English, but there is a danger that the play can sound like a mock epic, or that Medea can sound like a 1950s Radio 4 matron. My feeling is that each performer should use any regional accent with which she feels most comfortable and adapt the text using regional colloquialisms as necessary.

In *The Same Old Story*, Rame makes an attack on restrictive Italian abortion laws. In making the decision to transpose the character out of the Italian setting, I have had to drop the specific references to Italian laws. English law and medical practices, while being more liberal than they are in Italy, are still far from embodying 'a woman's right to choose', so I have interpolated a paragraph which describes the difficulties a woman in England might have if she were trying to get an abortion.

GILLIAN HANNA

A Woman Alone

*The light comes up on a few pieces of set indicating the
dining room of a lower middle class flat.*

*On stage, a long table on which are an iron, a radio, a basin
and a brush – all in a chaotic jumble. In front of the table, a
stool. Nearby, a small piece of furniture on top of which is a
tray with plasters, bandages, ointments, surgical spirit. A rifle
is hanging on the wall.*

*There are three entrances: the one at the back leads to the
kitchen, the stage left to the bedroom, and the third one,
stage right, is the front door.*

*A woman enters holding a basket overflowing with garments
to be ironed. She wears a low cut negligée. The radio is
blaring rock music. The woman, dancing frenetically, puts
the basket on the table. She grabs a man's jacket out of the
basket, and, still dancing, goes towards an imaginary
window at the front of the stage. She shakes the jacket as if
she's trying to get the dust out of it. She stops, pleasantly
surprised to find someone in the building opposite.*

WOMAN: (*at the top of her voice, to get attention*) Hey!
Hello there! Morning! How long have you been living
over there? I didn't even notice you moving in . . . I
thought it was empty . . . I'm thrilled to bits (*Almost
shouting.*) I was saying I'm thrilled to . . . Can't hear me?
Oh yeah, of course . . . the radio . . . I'll turn it off. I
always have to have the radio going full blast when I'm at
home on my own . . . otherwise I feel like sticking my
head in the oven . . . I've always got the stereo going in
this room . . (*Moves to stage right door. She opens the*

door. We hear music.) Can you hear? (*Closes the door.*)
And I've got the cassette machine in the kitchen . . .
(*Same business at the kitchen door.*) Can you hear? (*She
closes the door.*) So whatever room I'm in, I've always got
company. (*She goes over to the table and begins to work:
she brushes the man's jacket, sews on buttons etc.*) No .
not in the bedroom, that'd be a bit over the top! No I've
got the telly on in there   . it's always on – I keep it
turned right up! There's a church service on right now
. . . they're singing .   . in Greek, I think .   . that's what
Prince Philip talks, isn't it? What a weird language .
it's all double dutch to me   . Yeah, I like music you
can't dance to as well .   anything as long as it's music
. the sound keeps me company. What do you do for
company? Oh you've got a son! Aren't you the lucky one!
Come to think of it, I've got a son too! Actually, I've got
two kids .   . Sorry, I got so excited about talking to you,
I forgot about the other one   . No they don't keep me
company. The big girl's grown up. You know how it is,
she's got 'friends her own age'   . the little boy's still
with me, but he's no company .   well, he's asleep all
the time! He does nothing but sleep! He poos, he sleeps
and he snores! Oh I'm not moaning, I'm really well-off
here in my flat   . . I've got everything I could ever want
    My husband treats me like porcelain! I've got
everything! I've got   . . O God, I've got so much .   .
I've got a fridge! Yes I know everyone's got a fridge, but
(*Emphasising this.*) mine makes round ice cubes!! I've got
a washing machine   twenty-four programmes! It
washes *and* dries . . . ooh, you should see the way it
dries! Sometimes I have to wet everything again so I can
iron it . . . it comes out bone dry! I've got a non-stick
slow cooker   . a Magimix with all the attachments . .
music in every room .   what more could I ask of life?
I'm only a woman after all! Yes, I used to have a cleaning
lady but she ran away; then I got another one and she ran
away too . . . those women all run away from my house
. .   What? Oh no, not because of me
(*Embarrassed.*) It's my brother-in-law   Well he gropes

them! He feels them up! All women! He's a groper! . .
He's sick . . off his head? Well, I don't know if he's off
his head . . all I know is he wanted to do these things to
those girls . . and they weren't too keen – quite right
too. You should see it, love. There you are, minding your
own business, getting on with the housework, and
suddenly oops! there's this hand right up your . . gives
you the creeps! And you should see my brother-in-law's
hand! Thank God he's only got the one! What happened
to him? An accident . . a car accident . . . Just imagine,
so young, only thirty, and every bone in his body broken!
He's in plaster from head to foot. They put him in the
plaster sitting down so he'd be more comfortable . .
they just left him a little hole so he can eat and breathe
          he can't really talk   he just mumbles something
every now and again . . . you can't understand a word
          His eyes were all right, so they didn't plaster over
them .   they left the eyes . . . and they left that bloody
wandering hand too . . nothing wrong with that . and
the other thing, that's all right too . . (*She stops,
embarrassed.*) I don't know how to put it . . we've only
just met . . I wouldn't like you to think badly of me .
well . . . he's all right 'down there' . You've no idea
how all right he is 'down there'! Much too all right! He's
always wanting to . . well you know what I mean .
yes, so he has to take his mind off it . he's always
reading . . he reads all the time . . 'educating himself'
. porno comics . . his room is full of those disgusting
magazines. You know, those ones with the naked women
. . . in weird positions!! They must be so uncomfortable!
Those poor girls! After one of those sessions, I bet they
have to put them in plaster just like my brother-in-law!
          those lumps of flesh . . all blown up in full colour
. looks like a butcher's advert! One day I picked one
up by accident and it put me right off my pork chops at
lunchtime . I wanted to throw up . . anyway, since all
the cleaning women left I have to look after my brother-
in-law myself. I do it for my husband's sake you know
          well, he is his brother   What do you mean?

(*Indignant.*) I should say not! He respects me! And how!
Oh that'd be too much! He always asks first! Before he
lays a finger on me, he always asks permission first! (*The
telephone rings.*) Oh that must be my husband . . . he
always phones me around this time . . . Excuse me a
minute . . . (*Answering the phone.*) Hello? . . . What?
. . Yes but what . . . Fuck off you bastard! (*She bangs
the receiver down. She is furious. She smiles at the
neighbour across the way as if to ask forgiveness.*) Pardon
my French . . when you have to, you have to, don't
you? (*She starts work again – nervously.*) No, no it wasn't
my husband . . whatever next! No I don't know who it
was . . some pig who's always phoning me up . . one
of the dirty raincoat brigade . . he phones once, twice,
three times . . a thousand times a day . . he says filthy
things to me . . words . . . that aren't even in the
dictionary . . . I went and looked them up . . they're
not in it . . Sick? Listen, I've already got one sicko to
deal with . . I'm not going to start playing nursemaid to
every dirty old man in the country! (*Phone rings again.*)
That'll be him again! He wants to know what I'm doing
now . . I won't even let him get a word in! . . . (*Picks
up the receiver.*) Hello pig! I'm warning you, the police
have got this phone tapped and if . . (*Complete change
of tone.*) Oh hello dear . . (*Turns to neighbour, tapping
the telephone with her hand.*) It's my husband! (*Speaks
into the phone.*) No I wasn't getting ratty at you dear .
I thought you were . . well there's this bloke who's
always phoning me . . he asks about you . . . he says
you owe him money . . . so to give him a fright I just
dropped the word 'police' . . (*Complete change of tone.
Amazed! And more amazed!*) Yes I'm at home .
Bryan, I swear to you I'm at home! Look I'm sorry, but
what number did you dial? . . And so if I pick up the
phone, then where the hell do you think I am? I haven't
gone out! How could I go out when you lock me in the
flat?! (*Turns to the neighbour.*) What a husband, love!
. (*Into the phone.*) Hello . . no I'm not talking to
anyone.

Yes I said 'love' . I was talking to myself . . every
now and then, just to myself, I call myself 'love' . . No,
there's no one in the house Yes, your brother's here
but he's in the other room . . . yes, the baby's asleep .
Yes I fed him . Yes I put him on the potty . . (*Dry.*)
Yes, your brother as well! (*Tries to control herself.*)
Who's getting ratty? I was only telling you you could put
your mind at rest because everyone in the house has been
on the potty . . . Bye Yes Bryan, I'm happy . . I'm
very happy (*Getting more agitated.*) I was just standing
here doing the ironing roaring with laughter .
(*Shouting.*) I'M H-A-A-A-APPY!! (*She slams the phone
down. A shout of rage at the phone. After a moment the
phone rings again. She answers, it is the husband.*) Bryan
. . what if he turns up here? The man about the money?
(*To herself.*) What bloke about the money? Oh the one
who keeps phoning me up, yeah . . I have to pretend
I'm not in . turn off the radio, the stereo . . the telly
. . OK . whatever you say . . Ready for orders, Sir!
I tell you what I'll do for you: I'll go into the toilet, stick
my head down the bowl and pull the chain . now he's
going berserk . Oh go hang yourself! (*She puts down
the receiver. She is furious. She starts ironing again. Looks
towards the neighbour and forces a smile. After a while
she looks towards the back of the auditorium. Then she
turns back to the neighbour.*) Pardon me a minute. (*At the
top of her voice – she's looking above the neighbour.*) I
can see you, pig! I can see your binoculars catching the
sun! (*She looks for something to cover her breasts. She
covers the left one with the bib she's been ironing and the
right one with the iron.*) Oh my God!! (*To the neighbour.*)
I've ironed my breast! Up there, you can't see him, it's
the window above yours . . that's all I needed today –
that wanker! He stands up there and watches me. A poor
woman can't even put on something comfortable to do a
bit of ironing in her own home . . What am I supposed
to do? Put a macintosh on to do the ironing? (*Shouting at
the Peeping Tom*) And a balaclava! . . . And skis! . . . I
don't even know how to ski . . I'd fall A over T and

smash myself up like my brother-in-law! (*To the neighbour.*) The police? No I can't call the police. What do you think would happen then? They'd get here and start giving me the third degree . . 'Just how dressed or undressed were you at the time, Madam?' . 'Are you sure you weren't leading him on, Madam?' . . 'Pardon me for saying so, but this sounds very much like a case of striptease . ' And then it'd end up with them charging me with obscene behaviour likely to cause a breach of the peace in my own home! No, no . . I'll deal with him myself. (*Takes the rifle off the wall and aims it at the Peeping Tom. Shouting.*) Come on, pig! This'll put a curl in your tail! (*Disappointed.*) Oh, he's gone! Show him a rifle and he does a bunk! Coward! Come on, come on, come out of your sty you blind git and bring your bloody binoculars with you! (*Puts the rifle on the table. To the neighbour.*) Did I give you a good laugh? Do you think I'm off my trolley? . (*Starts ironing again.*) Better to be off my trolley than do what I was doing before . . . you should've seen me . every couple of months I'd swallow a bottle of sleeping pills . . I'd swallow anything . . any little round pills I could find in the bathroom . the baby's fluoride tablets . . . even the cat's worm pills . I was so desperate! Or I'd cut my wrists – I did that three months ago . . . yes my wrists . . Look, look here, I've still got the scars . . . Can you see? (*Shows her wrists.*) No, I don't think I can tell you that little tale well it's very private . . personal . I don't feel . well we've known each other such a short time. (*Complete change of tone.*) Shall I tell you? . . No. No . I've had a go at trusting people in your building! Oh well . . maybe it would do me a bit of good . . Get it off my chest . . . it's a sad story! All right then . . . It was all because of this boy . . fifteen years younger than me . . and he looked even younger than he was . . sort of shy and awkward . . . nice . . . soft . . . the sort of lad that if you went to bed with him you'd feel you were committing . . incest! Incest! Well I did it! What did I do? Incest! I went to bed with the boy! And do you know what the worst thing was? I wasn't even ashamed of myself . . . In fact I was on top of the world! I used to sing morning noon and night . . well not at night . . . at night I used to cry . . . 'You're depraved,' I'd say to myself . . (*Sound of a trumpet blowing off-stage.*) Excuse me a moment. It's my brother-in-law . . he blows his trumpet to let me know he wants me. Don't go away . . . I'll be back in a tick . . (*Putting her head round the stage right door.*) What is it dear? Be good for a bit will you, I'm having a chat with a friend of mine . . . (*Another ferocious blast drowns her words.*) Bastard! (*To the neighbour.*) If you only knew the filthy things he's saying with that trumpet! I swear when they take the plaster off I'll break and rebreak every bone in his body! And I'll do the same to my old man while I'm at it! Did you hear him just now on the phone? He said that when he comes home he's going to give me a good belt round the face! Me? My old man give me a slap round the face? Me? (*Starts ironing again.*) He says he does it because he loves me. 'I only do it because I adore you! You're still just a little child and I've got to look after you' . His idea of looking after me is to beat me up! He beats me to Kingdom Come and then he wants to go to bed with me and he couldn't care less about me . . . If I want to . . I always have to be ready! Be prepared! Like the Girl Guides! Instant sex! Like Nescafé! Warm, washed, willing and waiting . . . but shtum! As long as I'm still breathing that's all he's worried about . . . Oh and I have to do a bit of moaning now and again so he thinks I'm really into it . well to be quite honest, I'm not really into it . . . As a matter of fact I'm not into it at all . . I don't feel anything . . Not with my husband anyway I can't . . . I can't . . . have . . . (*She is very embarrassed. She can't find the right word. The neighbour says it for her.*) Yes, that's it . . that's the word! What a word! What a word! I never say it! Orgasm! Sounds like some horrible monster . . a cross between a monkey and an open sandwich . . . Orangutang and smörgåsbord . . . I can see the headlines now: 'Fully grown orgasm escapes

from London Zoo' . . . 'Nun poisoned by salmonella
infected orgasm in Danish restaurant' . . . and you know
when they say . . . 'He reached orgasm' . . . well I always
picture some poor old bloke tottering down the road and
just managing to hop on a bus! . . (*She laughs.*) Same
for you too? . . O.R.G.A.S.M. . . !!! What a wo-o-o-
rd! With all the names of things there are around, why
couldn't they have called it something else? What about
'chair'? . . . yes, 'chair' . . . so you could just say . . . 'I
had a chair' . . . for starters, no-one'd know you'd been
doing dirty things . . and also, when you got tired, you
could have a sit down! (*She laughs. She is much amused.*)
Where was I? . . . Sorry, all this stuff about orgasms
made me lose my thread . . . I feel nothing with my
husband! Nothing! Look, this is how I do it with him .
(*She's sitting down. Remaining seated, she goes rigid:
hands at her sides, legs straight out . like a soldier at
attention.*) And when he's finished I say, 'At ease!' No,
not out loud, he might thump me . . . to myself . . . I'm
always talking to myself . . . 'At ease!' . . and then I can
relax and go to sleep . . . I don't know why I don't feel
anything . . . maybe it's because I feel . . . frozen . . . I
feel as if I'm . . (*She can't find the right definition. The
neighbour suggests it to her. Complete change of tone.*)
Yes! How come it took you so long to move in over
there? Now I come to think . . . there's another word .
'USED' . yes, I'm 'used', like an electric razor or a
hairdryer . . but you see the other thing is that I didn't
have much experience when it came to sex . . I only had
two . . with my husband, which doesn't count, and
another one when I was still a kid . . . I was ten and he
was twelve . . . he was just a beginner! I hope he got
better at it when he grew up! . . . We didn't know
anything about all that stuff! All we knew was that babies
come out of your stomach . . . No I didn't feel anything
. . Not a thing! Just a terrible pain here. (*Indicates her
navel.*) Yes, here . . . my belly button. Yes well, you see
we thought that's where you did it . . so he was pushing
at me with his thingie: pushing and pushing! I had a sore

belly button for God knows how long afterwards . .
(*Laughing*.) . . . My Mum thought I'd caught chicken pox
again! I never told my husband the story about the belly
button . . . Well no . . Maybe ten years later he'd pick a
fight over it: 'Shut your face! What about that business
with the belly button . . Slag!!' No, no, I kept my mouth
shut. I told the priest . . . in confession . . . he told me
not to do it again . . Then I grew up . . . No I never had
another sexual experience . . well I didn't get much out
of that belly button stuff . . . I grew up. I got engaged
and my girl friends explained everything to me . . The
day of the wedding I was beside myself . . . I was singing
at the top of my voice . . . No, no, not out loud . .
inside . . I do everything inside . . I was singing inside
. . . 'Love is in the air . . . oho . . . mmn hmmn . . love
is in the air . . . ' (*Complete change of tone.
Disappointed.*) But no. It was my husband in the air!! Oh
the 'first night' was awful . . 'You've got to be kidding!
. . . Is that all there is to it?' . . I said to myself .
Ooh that first night was awful . . . well so was the
hundredth come to that . . . Find out? Find out? Who
was I supposed to ask? Then I started to read women's
magazines and I did find something out! (*Very self
important.*) I found out that we women have erogenous
zones! The spots where you feel the most when a man
touches you! . . (*Disappointed.*) Oh you know already
. you know a lot of things, don't you? Bloody hell, can
you believe the number of erogenous zones we've got! In
this one magazine they had a picture of a naked woman
cut up into four . . . you know, like one of those posters
you see in the butcher's, with a cow cut up into joints . .
like a map . . And all the erogenous zones were painted
in the wildest colours – depending on how sensitive they
are . . . so the haunch was bright scarlet! And this bit
here, behind your neck – what the butcher calls 'best end'
. . was purple . . and the fillet . . (*Complete change
of tone.*) Have you noticed how much fillet has gone up?
. . . Oh yeah, sorry . . (*Returns to previous tone.*) Well
the fillet was tangerine colour! And then there was the

rump . . . Now there's a thing! Rump! Best of the lot!
Extra special! The rump is almost as good as the 'loin'.
Apparently if the man knows how to do it right, you'll get
erotic shivers out of your loin . . . well it's enough to
make you go 'pop'. Like being touched on your rib of
beef, that's your 'sartorious' muscle . . . or in the other
direction it's a crown roast! With my husband: no rump,
no loin, no fillet, no crown roast, no nothing . . .
Nothing! I didn't feel anything at all! But in the end I
stopped worrying about it because I thought all women
felt the same as me . . . Until I met the boy. Well this is
what happened: my eldest was almost grown up, and I
didn't have much to do, so I said to my husband: 'Listen,
I'm sick of being a housewife. I want to do something
that exercises my brain a bit. Learn a language. What
about Italian. If we ever go to Italy it'd be useful because
they never stop talking it over there!' So he said 'Fine!'
And he brought home this young feller who was studying
at the University. He was about twenty-six and he spoke
wonderful Italian. So we'd been going about three weeks
when it suddenly dawned on me that this young feller was
madly in love with me! . . . How did I know? Well, when
I was reciting a verb, if I was waving my arms round
looking for the word and I accidentally brushed his hand,
he'd start trembling all over! . . . And stammering the
Italian so badly I couldn't understand a single word he
was saying! Well, I didn't know anything about
'emotions'. All I knew was my brother-in-law ferreting up
my skirt, the telephone pig and my old man prodding
about night after night . . . I started feeling these little
explosions of love . . whoosh . . . whoosh . . . in my
stomach . . . Like a nervous tummy upset! So I said to
myself: 'You're on the slippery slope to sin, my girl!' I
stopped the Italian lessons! The boy took it ever so badly
. . . I'd go down every morning to do the shopping and
he'd be waiting for me in the hallway . . . terribly pale
and sad and wearing a white mac . . . he was so
handsome! He looked like a young Yul Bryner! He'd
look at me with that blue eye of his . . . no, no, he had

two eyes . . . that's just my way of speaking . . . blue eye
. . . and I'd say to him (*In a low voice.*) 'Go away! .
I'm not the right woman for you! . . . Go away! I'm
almost old enough to be your mother! Go and find a girl
your own age!' (*She's shouting.*) 'GO AWAY!!' . . That
really put the wind up him! And then one day he did
something – I'll never forget it – I came down to go
shopping like every other day . . . and he's not in the
hallway! I felt terrible! 'Well, it doesn't matter,' I said to
myself, 'I'll just have to get used to it' . . So I go out
into the square, here down below, and something catches
my eye . . . All the walls of the building were covered in
writing . . huge letters . . in red paint . . . and they
said 'I love you, Sharon' . . Sharon, that's me . . .
Actually he'd written '*Ti amo*' . . . He'd written it in
Italian, you see, so no one could understand it! I dashed
back into the house . 'I've got to forget . . I've just
got to forget . ' So to make me forget, I started to hit
the bottle! Campari! It's bitter! Bloody hell, that
Campari's so bitter! Why do they make it so bitter? I was
chucking it down like cough linctus . . And there I was
. . all on my own, full of bitter thoughts and bitter
booze! . . . The doorbell rings. Who is it? The boy's
mother! How embarrassing! She says: 'Please don't think
too badly of me, but I'm desperate! My son is dying for
love of you . . he won't eat, he won't sleep, he won't
drink! You've got to save him! The least you can do is
come and see him' . . What was I supposed to do? I'm a
mother myself! So I go. He was in bed . . . pale, sad and
not wearing his mac . . As soon as he sees me he bursts
into tears . . and I burst into tears too . . and then his
mother bursts into tears too . . Then his mother goes
out. We're alone. (*She is very embarrassed.*) He hugs me
. I hug him . . . He kisses me . . I . . kiss him .
And then: 'Stop!!' . . That really shocked him. 'I've got
to talk to you . . I'm not ashamed of admitting that I
like you a lot . . . as a matter of fact I love you. (*Her
voice is getting louder and louder.*) I love you, I love you,
I loo-o-oo-ve you!!' . . Oh I was shouting my head off!

. It was the Campari!! (*Still shouting.*) 'I loo-o-o-ove
yo-o-o-ou!!' (*Change of tone.*) They told me later I was
shouting so loudly that all the people in the other flats
were hanging out of their windows trying to see what was
going on .   'Who's in love with who?' . 'Is it
someone up on the fourth floor who's in love?'   . 'No,
not in my place. I'm not in love with anyone'   What a
spectacle! Thank God no one knew who I was . . . (*Starts
shouting again.*) 'I love you. But I can't go to bed with
you. I've got two kids, a husband and a brother-in-law!'
So then he just jumps right out of bed – stark naked.
Bloody hell, was he ever naked! He grabs this knife and
holds it to his throat and says: 'If you won't go to bed
with me, I'll kill myself!' (*More embarrassed than ever.*)
Well, I'm not a murderess, right? Sacrifice the life of this
young man just to satisfy my own selfishness? I just
couldn't do it! So I ripped all my clothes off and I made
. . . (*Change of tone. Very sweet.*) Oh it was lovely!   .
Kisses . . strokes . . . Oh you should have been there!
Such kisses! .   Such caresses! God bless that knife! And
that's how I found out that love, LOVE, isn't that joke
with my husband . . . me underneath and him on top .
BANG . . . BANG .   BANG . . like a pile-driver!
Love is gentle and sweet .   . so sweet!

I went back the next day and the next day and the day
after that. Every day after every day after . . . Well, he
was ill, after all, wasn't he? And when I got back here to
the flat, I'd be like, stunned .   What do you mean,
'Why?' . . To get to my age and discover something I
thought only happened in the movies . . . when the old
man saw me in such a daze he thought I'd taken to the
bottle in a big way. He locked the Campari away! What a
berk! Then he began to get suspicious, so he had me
followed . . . I was in the boy's bedroom one day . . . I
was standing there naked . . . and he was standing there
naked too . . . and we were just saying hello to each
other . . 'How are you today?' 'I'm fine, thanks, how
about you?' . . . when the door bursts open and there's

my husband – fully dressed! I didn't know what to say, so I said 'Oh, hello, it's you, is it?' I mean it's not exactly something that happens to you every day of the week is it? Standing stark naked beside a strange man who's stark naked and your husband with his overcoat on! I wish I'd never opened my mouth! 'Yes, it's me-e-e-!! You peasant!' . He called me a peasant . . I wouldn't have thought that was the right word. Anyway, then he started shouting like a lunatic . and he was trying to throttle the boy . . and he was trying to throttle me at the same time . but my husband's only got two hands and no matter how hard he squeezed, he couldn't do it . though I was trying to help him . . . I was squeezing my own throat against the boy's and I'd stopped breathing too. My mouth was shut tight . Oh God, I wanted to die! Then suddenly my nose started breathing by itself . my nose has got a mind of its own! In rushed his mother, and then his sister and then his granny . . and I'm still standing there as naked as the day I was born with my nose doing its own thing . . I hurtle into the bathroom and shut the door behind me . . grab a razor blade and slash . slash . slash . I start slashing every vein I can lay hands on . . I'm searching for them . here's another one . slash! Another one – slash! It was a bloody massacre! I never knew we had so many veins! I was even cutting them lengthwise . so I'd die quicker! But my husband wanted to kill me personally, himself, so he put his shoulder to the door and broke it down . And when he saw me sitting there, covered in blood . it was so red . You know my blood is really bright red . he says to me: 'I'm not going to kill you any more . I'm going to take you to the hospital'. Then he wrapped me up in a nice bedspread – because he didn't want to mess up the car . he took me to the hospital . . then he forgave me . . . he's been terribly kind . But ever since then he's kept me locked up in the flat . . Solitary confinement . . Of course I know it's illegal . . Call the police? What's the matter with you? Got some sort of thing about calling the police? Got

a relative in the force or something? I can't call the police
. they'd get here and then the whole story of the boy
would come out for sure . . . and then there'd have to be
a legal separation. My husband would take the kids away
from me for sure and all I'd be left with would be the
brother-in-law and his wandering hand! No . . . no .
Look, I . . . (*The phone rings. She picks up the receiver.*)
Hello . . (*In a low voice. Very emotional.*) Sweetheart
. . why are you phoning me? (*Shouting to the
neighbour.*) It's the boy! (*The intimate tone again.*) Please
. . you mustn't phone me any more! How can I see you
when he keeps me locked up? . . You're going to break
in? How? . . . Don't you dare do any such . . . Hello .
hello . . . (*To the neighbour.*) He's hung up! He's gone
mad! He's off his head! He says he's going to come round
and break in – with a bent nail! . . . Of course I know he
won't be able to do it, but what do you think it's going to
look like if one of the neighbours passes by and sees him
fiddling at my door with a bent nail! (*A knocking at the
door.*) That's him! Bloody hell, that was quick!

(*She goes to the front door. She is terrified.*) Go away!!
My husband will be here any minute! . . . (*Change of
tone.*) Who are you? . . . Money? What money? (*To the
neighbour.*) This is a disaster! . . . It's the man about the
money! He says he's come to collect the debt! (*To the
door.*) There's no one at home . . . Yes I know I'm at
home, but . . . I'm the maid . . . Husband? Who
mentioned a husband? Oh did I? Well . . . my husband's
the cook here . . no the master and mistress aren't at
home . . they've gone on a cruise . . by car . . Look,
I've got orders not to open the door and not to speak to
anyone, and not to turn the radio or the stereo on . .
Anyway, I couldn't open the door even if I wanted to,
'cos I haven't got a key . . . (*Aside.*) . . Oh hell, what've
I said . . (*To the creditor.*) No, I haven't got the key
because . . . they lock me in . . . the mistress thinks I
steal things . . . so . . No, no, don't worry I'm not going
to starve to death . . . the larder's stuffed full of food .

Police? Why would you want to call the police? (*To herself.*) He must be related to that woman across the way . . . (*To the creditor.*) Hello! . . . Hey! Hello! (*Coming to the window.*) He's gone! . . He's gone to call the police . . I think he's bluffing . . . he just said that to give me a fright . (*More knocking at the front door.*) There's someone else knocking . . who's it going to be this time? The debt collector, the police or the crazy boy? I'm not going to answer, whoever it is . . . (*Louder knocking.*) What do you bet it's the police? (*We can hear shouting: 'Sharon . . . Sharon'.*) My husband! (*She goes to the door.*) Bryan! Why are you banging like that? I know the bell's broken, but you've got the keys . . . why don't you open the door? . . Lost the keys? . . Oh Jesus, now what'll happen to me? I'll starve to death, walled up alive like the Count of Monte Cristo . . . walled up for ever, me and the baby and the wandering hand . . . what a way to die! Oh my God, what a way to die! (*To the husband.*) Listen, your friend was here . . . yes, the one about the money . . . and he went to call the police . . No he didn't talk to me – I'm not a complete idiot – he talked to the maid . . What maid? We haven't got a maid? Of course you've got a maid! A maid, a nurse, a baby-sitter, a charlady, do-all, wash-all, fucked-up and fucked-over! I'm not hysterical . . . I haven't gone crazy . . I'm thrilled the police are on their way and we can be finished with all this . . . finished once and for all . . Yes, shove off . . . and don't come back . . . ever!! You . . (*She is beside herself. She is searching for a rude name to call her husband.*) dyslexic!! (*She realises what she has said. She is mortified. To the neighbour.*) When I think of all the dirty words I know, and I have to go and call him 'dyslexic'! . . and he reads perfectly! I made a complete fool of myself! I really gave it to him, though, didn't I? (*A wail from the baby . . . she is terrified.*) The baby's crying! Oh my God, what'll I do? He's never woken up like that – not since he was born! (*She runs to the stage right doorway.*) What the hell are you doing in my bedroom? . Filthy brute . You woke the baby

up just to get me in here . . . what are are you up to
now? . . . Pack it in will you? Stop pulling me about like
that! Let me go! (*Wail from the baby.*) Shush, sssshh, be
good, sweetie pie. (*The phone rings.*) Bastard! You've
ripped my negligée – and it's only just arrived from
Littlewoods . . . I'm coming, dammit . . I'll deal with
you when your brother gets back, you wait and see . . . if
he ever comes back. (*Goes to answer the phone.*) Hello
. . . (*She is furious.*) Listen, enough is enough. If you
don't stop all this crap, one of these fine days I'm going to
go right off my head . . I'll put . . a bomb down the
phone! I'll blow up your gums!! Bastard! You ought to be
ashamed of yourself! I'm a mother! How would you like
it if some dirty old man kept phoning your white haired
old mother up? There she is, knitting quietly by the fire
and some rotten pig is spewing all the filth at her that you
spew at me . . . how would you like someone to treat
your mother like that? Ah, that shut him up! I've finally
found something that appeals to his sense of decency!
(*Pause. She puts the phone down.*) He's an orphan! (*She
shouts abuse at the phone.*) Pig! Bastard! Swine! (*To the
neighbour.*) Look what the brother-in-law's done to me,
love . . and he's woken the baby up . . hello
(*Calling.*) . . Hello . . . (*The baby starts to cry again
. . . she is disappointed.*) Oh she's gone . . (*Looks up.*)
Oh the wanker's back though! (*Raises her voice to talk to
stage right door.*) Sweetie pie . . (*Picks up the rifle.*)
Now Mummy's going to show you how to kill a wanker
. (*There's a knocking at the front door.*) Don't move
an inch . . I'll come back and kill you in a couple of
minutes . . (*Goes to door.*) Who is it? For God's sake
go away . . . my husband will be here any minute and so
will the police and someone looking for money .
(*There's something fiddling in the lock.*) Don't you touch
my lock with that nail! Anyway, you'll never get in . .
I'm putting the chain on . . . (*She does so.*) Help! (*Runs
to the table.*) Hello! . . . Yoo hoo! . . . Oh thank God
you've come back! It's the crazy boy! He's managed to
open the door! No he can't get in because I've put the

safety chain on . . Yes I'll tell him now . . (*Goes to the door. Stops dead at the sight of the boy's hand which is poking in through the gap in the doorway.*) Get the hell out of my house with that hand of yours! . . . (*The hand makes insistent signs that she should come closer.*) What do you want? . . To shake my hand? Why can't you get it through your thick head – my husband's going to turn up any minute . . . (*He insists.*) . . God you don't give up, do you?! All right then but hurry up . . (*She gives him her hand . . the boy tries to pull her towards him.*) What are you pulling me for? I'll never get through that crack . . (*The baby wails.*) Let me go, there's the baby crying . . I've got to feed him . . Go away now . (*She frees herself from the boy's grip and goes to the kitchen door.*) And lock the door behind you with your bent nail . . Actually, leave it with the caretaker, will you, 'cos my husband's lost his keys. (*To the baby.*) Now then, sweetie pie, I'll get you something to eat . (*Going into the kitchen, she sees that the boy's hand has stayed where it was. She picks up a large plastic spoon.*) Go away . . Look, I'm getting to the end of my tether. If you're not careful, I'm going to make you really sorry . . (*Threatening.*) Watch out, I'm going to stab you with this spoon . . . I'll cut all your fingers off . . Don't believe me? (*She goes to the boy and slashes him hard on the hand with the spoon. He screams. She's appalled. Looks at the spoon and then runs to the window.*) I've stabbed him with a spoon!! . . . What shall I do? Take out a patent? What are you talking about?! Disinfect it? Yes of course, you're right, I'll have to disinfect it . . Yes I've got some . . my husband gives me everything . (*Picks up the surgical spirit which is on the tray and runs to the boy.*) Keep still . . . No it won't hurt . . it's what they use on kids . . Oh sweetheart, sweetheart . . Look what I've done to you! I'm a murderess! Forgive me! Now go away . . A kiss? On the lips? No, I'm not giving you anything on the lips! No I'm sorry, I'm not taking the chain off! But I couldn't get my head through the crack! What about my ears? Oh God, you really don't give up, do you!? (*She puts her head through the crack in the door.*) Let go now . . . let go . . . Oh bloody hell! My head! My head's stuck in the door! Push! Push! Not with your lips you idiot! With your hand! (*She gets her head out of the door with great difficulty.*) Ooh that hurts! (*She takes a couple of steps away from the door. The boy starts knocking frantically at the door.*) That's enough!! This is no time to start playing jazz! (*The boy tries to pull his arm out of the door. He can't.*) Go away! What's up now? . Oh bloody hell! . . . (*She runs to the window.*) Oh my God, he's got his arm stuck in the door! He'll be there for life! They'll have to deliver his pension to him in my doorway! . . . My husband will slaughter me! What'll I do? . . . Oh yes . . . water . . . and soap . . . like you do with rings . . . (*Goes towards the Peeping Tom's window.*) Sod off! (*To the neighbour.*) I'll use hot water, that'll be better . . . (*She picks up the bowl on the table. To the Peeping Tom. She is exasperated.*) You lesbian shirtlifter!!! (*She's bustling about the room.*) Now then . . a wave for the wanker . . . hot water for the wounded . . mush for the baby . . (*Trumpet blast from the brother-in-law.*) . . and a grope for the groper . (*The phone rings.*) And a phone call from the pigging phone pig! (*She goes to the phone.*) Hello pig! (*Change of tone. She thinks it's the husband.*) Hi! What? Who are you? . . . I'm sorry, I thought you were my husband . No my husband isn't here . . . if you'd like to tell me . Yes . . Yes . . . (*She laughs to herself.*) Do you want to know what I think? Congratulations and I hope they're all boys! . . Look, I think you must have the wrong number . . Yes a man does live here, he happens to be my husband and the only person he gets pregnant is me! . . No? He's got your daughter pregnant too? No he hasn't mentioned it to me . . . what a pig! How old is your daughter? Sixteen? Listen, if you ask me, I think you should keep your sixteen-year-old daughter locked up at home instead of letting her wander the streets getting pregnant by other women's husbands! My husband keeps me locked up . . . look how old I am and he still keeps me locked up . . bastard! (*She hangs up. To the neighbour.*) He called me a tart! My husband gets his daughter pregnant and he calls me a tart!! (*The boy is trying to attract the woman's attention by knocking on the door.*) Leave me alone. I've got a family disaster on my hands! I've got a pregnant husband! (*She goes into the kitchen – returns with the bowl in one hand and the baby's food in the other.*) I'm coming, I'm coming . . . bloody hell, this stuff is scalding hot! (*Goes into the bedroom.*) Here I am, here I am sweetie pie . . . stay still you cretin . . . stop pulling at me . . be careful, this is boiling hot! (*We hear a scream from the brother-in-law.*) Bloody hell! (*She re-enters.*) You'll never guess what I've done, love . I poured the baby's boiling mush in his eyes . . . no, not the baby's . . my brother-in-law's!! . . . What'll I do? (*Goes to the bedroom and brings the brother-in-law in. He is a dummy, completely covered in plaster and sitting in a wheel chair. To the neighbour.*) Germolene? . of course, yes, I'll put some Germolene on it . . . yes . . yes . . of course I've got Germolene, my husband gives me everything . . (*To the boy who's knocking again.*) Leave me alone! I've scalded my brother-in-law! (*Takes the ointment off the tray and runs to the wheelchair.*) Here I am . . . oh dear, is it burning? Well you would go and do it! I warned you I was holding the baby's food . . give over with that hand . . (*The brother-in-law manages to pull her to him and holds onto her tightly.*) Let go of me! Let go of me! (*She tries to free herself without success. She is furious.*) I'll throw this boiling water all over you! (*The brother-in-law lets go.*) Oh the penny's dropped at long last, has it? (*She runs to the boy with the bowl.*) Quick, put your hand in the bowl . . . no, no it's not boiling . . . I only said that to frighten the brother-in-law . . (*The boy puts his hand in the bowl. The water is boiling. He screams and quickly retracts his arm.*) Oh it was boiling! Well at least you've got your arm back! . Now go away . You've scalded yourself? Well, put some of this ointment on it . . (*She passes the ointment to him through the door. We gather*

*that the boy has grabbed her hand and is trying to
masturbate with it . . . she tries to free herself but cannot.
She is indignant.*) What are you up to? Let go of me .
Have you gone crazy? . . Let go of me!! If anybody sees
this we'll be carted off to the police station, door and all!
Let go of me! You've got a bloody nerve! Show a bit of
respect, will you . . if you don't stop I'll make you sorry
. I'll really make you sorry . Oh you don't believe
me, huh? Well I'll show you! . . (*Mimes pulling him
violently towards her and then slams the door. Scream
from the boy who runs off. The woman is in despair. She
takes the chain off the door and opens it wide. Goes sadly
to the table and starts to talk to the neighbour again.*) I
punished him . well he really let me down, that one
. . I thought he was LOVE . but he's not . . he's a
pig like all the rest of them . . . (*She is desperate.*) I can't
take any more of this . . (*She hears the baby crying.*) I
just can't take any more . My baby . . I must go and
see to the baby . he's the only one I really love
(*She makes as if to go into the bedroom, but she's stopped
by the phone ringing. And the brother-in-law has started to
blow his trumpet again.*) Shut up! Shut up! You cretin!
Shut it! Just bloody shut it!! (*Baby screaming, phone
ringing, brother-in-law trumpeting . . all getting louder
and louder in unison . . She can no longer control
herself.*) That's it! That's enough! (*Takes the rifle and
points it at her throat.*) I'm going to kill myself!! I'm going
to kill myself!!! . (*Total silence for a few seconds. The
neighbour says something to her. The woman listens
attentively.*) Yes . . yes . . (*She can hardly keep back
the tears.*) Yes! (*She puts the rifle on the table.*) What was
I thinking of? ... . Oh God . . Oh God . . Thank you,
love . Thank God you came to live opposite . Yes,
I'll do it straight away . . you give such good advice! (*A
blast from the brother-in-law.*) Yes, chuck I'm coming
. I'm all yours! Come on! (*Happy trumpet.*) Come on
then . (*She wheels the chair to the front door.*) Let's
take you for a nice little sexy walk! (*She shoves him out of
the door. Huge thump. Then a series of trumpetings and*

thumps.) Mind the glass door! (*The sound of glass
smashing.*) One down!!   . (*Wail from the baby. The
woman goes towards the bedroom. She stops in the middle
of the stage. Looks at the Peeping Tom .   . Smiles at him
languidly. Greets him. Slowly goes to the table, moving
very sexily   . . she blows him kisses. All of a sudden she
snatches up the rifle and fires at him.*) The wanker wanks
no more! Two down!!   .   (*She is going to her son but
she's stopped by the phone ringing. She answers in a voice
like thunder.*) Hello!! (*Change of tone.*) Bryan?! (*Almost
sweetly.*) Yes, I'm fine   . yes, yes, everything's very
peaceful up here   . yes you can come up .   . I'm
waiting for you   (*She hangs up. To the neighbour.*) No
love, don't worry .   I'm calm .   . I'm very calm .
(*Leans on the table, pointing the rifle at the front door.*)
I'm just waiting .   very calmly

Blackout.
Music.

                    translated by GILLIAN HANNA

Rise and Shine

A bed-sit: a double bed, a bedside table with an alarm clock and a small lamp, a cupboard, a sideboard, various tins and jars, a table, a gas cooker, a fridge, a washing machine, a sink. There is also a cot with a baby, represented by a large doll, in it.

A man and a woman are asleep on the bed. The man can be represented by a large puppet, as he has no lines. In the semi-darkness we can see that the woman appears to be having a nightmare.

Three pieces, one weld, slam down the drill . . . two bolts, one weld, slam down the cutter . . . (*She screams.*) O Christ! I've sliced my fingers off! My fingers . . . Help me to pick them up will you . . . the boss won't like this . they're messing everything up! (*She wakes up with a start . . but she's still in the nightmare.*) My fingers! I won't be able to pick my nose any more . . . (*She looks at her hand.*) I've still got them!! It was just a dream! Bloody hell, now I can't even sleep without dreaming about work! As if I didn't get enough of it in the factory. What's the time? (*She looks at the clock.*) Half past six? (*She gets out of bed, turns on the light and quickly puts on slippers and dressing-gown.*) The sodding thing didn't go off!! O Jesus, I'm so late. (*She runs to the cot and picks up the baby.*) Come on kiddo, wakey wakey! Let's get the day on the road! (*Goes to the table which is near the sink.*) Ups-a-daisy, come on then Mummy's little beauty, let's get up and at it! Wee! You've weed yourself again and I only changed you three hours ago. You pissing little pisspot . . . And I'm in such a hurry. We'll have to run all the way to the nursery 'cos if we get there after seven they'll send us straight back home! (*She undresses the baby.*) Now Mum's gonna wash your little botty . . . (*She turns the tap on.*) Hot water . . . O hell there's no hot water. What do you bet that thick git Steve turned the boiler off last night? No, no he's not that thick, here's the hot water now . . . (*Picks the baby up and goes to the sink.*) Now let's wash that little mush. Sh sh sh! Don't make a racket or you'll wake Pops up . . . we'll let him have another half hour's kip, lucky sod! Then he'll have to whizz off to Metal Box . . Wheeeeeeeeee! (*She realises that she was screaming, so she screams again, but under her breath.*) Wheeee! Leg it to the bus, jump on the train, whoosh into the factory. (*Puts the baby on the table and dries it with a towel.*) And on with the dance, just like the chimpanzees' tea party, Daddy on the production line (*She mimes the production line.*) hop two three four, hop two three four . (*She laughs.*) Ho, ho so you think that's very funny, do you kiddo . . . like having a performing monkey for a Mum, do you then? There, that's got you nice and dry . . (*Picks up a tin of talcum powder.*) A nice little dusting down . . (*She realises she's made a mistake.*) with grated cheese!! Who the hell put grated cheese in the talc tin? O Christ what a mess! Wait I'll get it off you . . this stuff costs a fortune . . Oh well, waste not want not . . (*She mimes getting the grated cheese off the baby's bottom.*) At least you can say my baby's bottom is clean enough to eat your dinner off! (*She dresses the baby – fast.*) Come on, come on, my little piss artist. There we are! All done! What time is it? O Jesus it's so late! Stay still a minute while your Mum has a bit of a splash too. (*Goes to the sink, mimes turning on the tap, and soaping her face and hands. She sings.*) 'Now faces that do dishes can be soft as your hands . . ' Water! The water's run out! Bleedin bloody hell! A family like this in a place like this and three hundred other families like this . And everyone takes it into their stupid heads to have a wash at the same time! How am I supposed to rinse this off now? Shit! Now I've got soap in my eye. (*She grabs a towel and wipes the soap out of her eye.*) Well I can have a wash some other time, it's not going to make any difference to

me . (*Runs a quick comb through her hair.*) No one
looks at me twice any more anyway . . they do smell me
though . . I'll have a quick squirt under the arms. (*Picks
up the aerosol can.*) Whoever invented aerosols should get a
bloody medal! Let's have a quick squirt . . (*She does so.*)
Ouch, that stings! What the hell is it? (*Reads the can.*)
Radiator paint! I've got a bleedin silver armpit!! How'm I
going to get this off? I'll have to find some white spirit when
I get to the factory. (*She gets dressed fast, picks up the child,
wraps it in a blanket and goes to the door.*) Get a bloody
move on, come on, come on, get moving. It's twenty to
seven. We'll just make it. Let's get Mum's handbag . . .
Mum's jacket . . . (*Goes to the door. Stops.*) The key? The
key? Where did I put the key? Every morning it's the same
performance with the damn key. You'd think I had all the
time in the world, the hours I spend ferreting around for
that key. (*She searches frantically through her pockets. She
looks round.*) Keep calm. Let's have a bit of calm. Let's just
try and go over everything I did last night. Now then . . I
got home and Steve wasn't here . . I opened the door. The
baby was in Mum's right hand and the handbag and the key
were in Mum's left hand. I put the handbag down here .
(*Points to the table.*) and I put the baby in the cot . . I go
back outside. I pick up the shopping bag. I've still got the
key in my hand. The carton of milk's under my arm . . I
come back inside . . . I put the bag down here and the milk
in the fridge. The fridge. What do you bet I put the key in
the fridge. (*Goes to the fridge and opens it.*) No, not there.
Not in the egg compartment, not in the butter dish . . I
didn't put the milk in here either . . . I put the lemon-
scented liquid Ariel in here. Well that's right. You got to
put lemons in the fridge otherwise they go off! I'm crazy!
I'm completely crazy!! I must've put the milk in the washing
machine! (*She looks in the washing machine.*) Not there.
Thank God. Where did I put the milk then? On the cooker
. yes that's right, for the baby's cereal. That's right. I
needed both hands free to open the carton of milk so I put
the key in my mouth . . and who knows why the hell I put
the key in my mouth and not on the table? And then I lit

the gas . . . so: the baby's milk is on the gas cooker, I light
the baby, I mean I light the milk . . . I light the gas! I leave
the milk there to heat up and I discover the baby .   . I
mean I take his covers off . . . his clothes . . . (*She goes to
the cot, miming what she's describing.*) I get the baby and I
put him on the table   . no I don't. I keep hold of the baby
and I go over to the cupboard and take out the baby bath
so's I can wash him   . . and I've still got the key between
my teeth .   . and I put the bath down here . . . and where's
the baby   . the baby's gone! Now I've lost the baby for
real. Where did I put the baby? (*She runs round the various
pieces of furniture she's talking about, opening the doors.*) In
the fridge . . . in the washing machine .   . in the cupboard!
I'd put the baby in the cupboard! Thank heavens he started
to cry otherwise God knows when I'd have found him! Poor
baba! I'd given meself such a fright I rushed over to get a
glass of water. (*She stops, appalled.*) You don't think I
swallowed the key? Of course .   well I still had it in my
mouth, didn't I? No I couldn't possibly have swallowed it,
my key's got a hole in it so I would have spent the whole
night whistling and Steve would have had a fit . . . So where
did I put the key? Let's just keep calm. No need to go
berserk. I pick up the baby bath and I go to fill it up with
warm water, I get the bicarb . . . (*Picks up jar.*) I always
put a couple of teaspoons of bicarb in the baby's bath water
. . . maybe it fell in the jar? (*Studies the contents of the jar.*)
Sugar!! Who put sugar in the bicarb jar   . . (*Looks at
another jar.*) and bicarb in the sugar jar. How long have I
been washing the baby in sugar? That explains it! That's
why the woman at the nursery said: 'I have to keep your kid
indoors .   . if I let him outside bees and wasps and flies
swarm all over him'. Poor baby! And Steve, he kicked up
such a fuss about the coffee . . . I must've put bicarb in it
. . . No wonder he was belching! Back to the key. Where
did I put the key? O God, I'm an idiot! Wrong! I got it all
wrong! I never took the key out of the lock . . . oh ye-e-es.
Because when I was giving the baby his bath I heard Steve
scrabbling about at the door because when I came in I
closed the door and left the key in the lock .   . so he

couldn't open it and he was going crazy, ranting and
swearing like a trooper.

I took the key out of the door . . . he came in . . . shouting
like a lunatic, and I'm sure I had the key in my hand .
and I went right up to him and I waved it under his nose
. . . I felt like poking one of his eyes out with it, and I said:
'So I left the key in the lock, want to make something of it?
So murder me then, wife-killer!!!' 'Give me a break' he said
'I'm not shouting about the key . . . it's that bloody train, it
was an hour late . . . an hour and a half to go ten miles .
And that's all unpaid time . . The boss doesn't pay me
travelling time to work, and he doesn't pay me travelling
time back from work and he doesn't pay me for the bus
journey. All that bloody traipsing about . . I'm not a
bloody tourist, am I?'

'So why are you taking it out on me?' I say to him, and I've
still got the key in my hand. 'Anyway the boss isn't called
"boss" any more. It's all "Multinational Conglomerate"
these days. We're all free as birds these days. The
Multinational Conglomerate boss screws you for your
travelling money and you go mad, but you don't go mad
over the money he screws ME for . yes, that's right, me,
because on top of working like a maniac eight hours for
him, I have to come home and be dogsbody for you free
gratis and for nothing! All for him, him, Mr Multibloody-
national Conbloodyglomerate!'

And then I gave the baby his milk. (*Goes to cot.*) I picked
him up . . (*She picks him up and searches round in the
cot.*) It could have fallen in here . . Oh Christ you've done
it again, you have, you've done it, you've gone and done it
again! Jesus H. Christ .   . (*Goes to the table near the sink.*)
How many times do I have to tell you, you wait till you get
to the nursery to dirty your nappy! You're supposed to do it
at two minutes past seven, just in time for the nurse to
change you! (*While she's talking, she quickly undresses the
baby and washes him.*) What's the time? Oh Jesus, it's late!
I'm not going to make it . . I'm not going to make it .

I'm going to lose the whole day   . Fuckin Ada look at
this .   I can't understand how such a tiny bottom can
produce such enormous shits!! (*While she washes the baby
she picks up the conversation with Steve.*) 'The family, this
sacred cow we call the family, was invented expressly so
that idiots like you can get themselves well knackered,
working like slaves on the production line all day, and then
come home at night to us maids-of-all-work. We're just
punchbags so you can get it all out of your system! (*She's
finished washing the baby. She dries him and gets him
dressed again.*) And we get you on your feet again for him.
For free! All so you can be ready for the next day; off you
go, fed and watered, bright-eyed and bushy-tailed, all ready
to produce more for Mr Multinational! He's God Almighty,
he is! He creates the boom, he creates the crash! First it's
deflation, then it's inflation. Then it's a credit boom then a
credit squeeze. The pound crashes, then the euro-dollar
then the petro-dollar . . Then he shrugs his shoulders and
says . . "Well what can I do? It's just market forces .
Out of my control".' And Steve starts laughing, 'Well, well,
well .   . I never knew I had a loony feminist for a wife!
Since when have you been going to consciousness-raising
sessions? Going to burn our bra are we?' 'Listen dickhead' I
say 'I don't need to hang about with feminists to know that
this life we're living is a pile of shit! We both work like
galley slaves, never a moment to say two words to each
other, never a minute to ourselves. You never ask me:
"Are you tired? Can I give you a hand?" Who cooks the
meals? Me. Who washes the dishes? Me. Who does the
shopping? Me. Who turns cartwheels trying to make the
money stretch to the end of the month? Me, me, me!! But
I've got a job as well! Who washes your dirty socks? Me.
How many times have you washed my socks? And this is
what they call marriage? I want to be able to talk to you. I
want to LIVE with you, not just be in the same house as
you. Does it ever enter your thick head that I might have
problems too? Your problems are my problems, that's OK
by me .   . but I'd like my problems to be yours too, not
just yours are mine and mine are my own! I want to be able

to talk, talk to you . . . but when you get home from work you just pass out on the bed. Every evening: *television*!! Every Sunday: *The Big Match*! You're glued to twenty-two cretins running round in their underpants, crowding round a stupid ball and kicking each other in the shins, and there's some other wanker in the middle wearing his underpants as well, only this one's got a black jersey and a whistle!' So then Steve goes purple in the face, he's furious, you'd think I'd said something rude about his mother, and he shouts: 'And what the fuck do you think you know about sport?' Well that wasn't exactly the right answer, was it? So I lost my rag. I went berserk, I was shouting like a lunatic! It just all came out. I was shouting, he was shouting . . I got nasty, so he got nastier, then I got nastier still . . . and in the end I said: 'Well if this is marriage I think I've made a terrible mistake'. So I picked up my mistake . . . (*She picks up the baby and goes to the door.*) and I started to walk out. And I'm sure I had the key in my hand at that point . . . I know I had it, because I opened the door. Steve comes over to me . . . you should have seen his face, poor Steve, white as a sheet and really upset. I'd never made a scene like that before and he could see I wasn't joking . . . He pulls me back inside: 'Listen, don't be like this, wait   '

'Don't touch me!' 'Let's talk about it. Let's talk about it first, and then if you still want to leave, well OK but let's talk first! We've got to discuss it, haven't we? For God's sake, we've got to discuss it!' So he was nudging me towards the 'discussion'. (*Points to the bed.*) And he makes me sit down, and he says yes, I was right . . . but he was used to being spoiled by his MOTHER . . . and he treated me like his MOTHER . . . but he was wrong, he was going to change . . . in fact he was well into the famous so-called SELF-CRITICISM . . . and he did it so well . . . he was so sweet . . . that I started to cry! And the more self-criticism he did the harder I cried, and the harder I cried, the more self-criticism he did! I had a really good cry last night! What about the key? (*She suddenly remembers.*) Of course! He took it off me, I'm sure he did, and he put it in his jacket pocket. (*Grabs the jacket, rummages in the pockets.*) Here it is! My key! And his! What time is it? Quarter to seven . . . I can still make it . . Come on, let's get our skates on, I can still make it . . . (*Picks up the baby and starts frantically running round.*) Mum's baby, Mum's jacket, Mum's handbag, (*She's ready to leave. She suddenly stops.*) the bus pass . . (*She puts the baby on the table.*) Wait a sec, kiddo, let me just get out the bus pass now, the bus is bound to be packed to the gills, and if I have to put you down everyone'll tread on you . . (*Ferrets round in the bag.*) Here it is . . (*She looks at it amazed.*) Six holes? Six holes for going and six for the return journey! (*She's gobsmacked.*) Six holes for going and six for the return journey! Who's been punching holes in my bus pass? Six holes . . What day is it? (*She looks at the calendar on the wall. She doesn't say anything . . She's amazed . . gobsmacked. She picks up the baby. Almost voiceless, she speaks.*) Sunday? (*Shouting.*) Sunday!! (*To the baby.*) Why didn't you tell me? It's Sunday! I must be off my bleedin' nut . . I wanted to go to work on Sunday! I'm crazy! It's Sunday! (*Singing.*) 'Sunday, sweet Sunday, with nothing to do . . . don't work on Sunday, just sleep hours through . . .' Back to bed, kiddo, back to bed. Sleepy time!! (*Putting the baby into the double bed and then coming downstage.*) I want to have a dream where every day of the week is Sunday! A whole lifetime of Sundays! It's the end of the world . . Everlasting Sunday has broken out! They've done away with all the other days of the week!! They've hanged Mondays . . . they've shot Thursdays . . . they've chopped Fridays into little pieces! . . . It's Sunday every day of the week! Bye-byes time kiddo! (*She runs to the bed and gets under the covers.*) Bye-byes! And if I have another dream about work, I'll personally strangle myself with my own bare hands! Sleep! (*On the last words she pulls the sheet up over her head.*)

Blackout.

translated by GILLIAN HANNA

Bless Me Father For I
Have Sinned

*As the lights come up, we see a confessional centre stage. It
is the only indication that the play takes place in a church.
A woman enters dressed in a costume that makes her look
like a gypsy/hippy. She is carrying an enormous bag. She
moves cautiously. We get the feeling that she is being
followed.*

Jaysus, Mary and Joseph and the blessed ass! . . . don't say
they're going to folly me right into the church! Now where
can I hide? .   . In the sacristy .   . Well now where's the
sacristy? This side of the choir or the other? (*She's trying to
find somewhere to hide all the while.*) Here's another two of
the bastards . . . Sweet Jaysus they've got me cornered now
. . . the confessional . . . I'll hide in the confessional .   .
(*Goes to enter the box, but she stops.*) There's someone in
there! There's a priest in there! Be God, these bloody
priests get in everywhere! Well I'll make a confession then,
so. Let's see if the polis have the neck to interrupt the Holy
Sacrament .   . (*She kneels down in the right hand side of
the box. She speaks under her breath.*) Hello . . . ummm
 . . I mean . . . Father . . . Father! God Almighty, he's
asleep! (*She knocks on the grille.*) Father, Father, wake up!
Oh at long last! Father I want to make a confession and I'd
like to do it quick if it's all the same to ya . . . What do ya
mean, it isn't possible . . . Oh he's fallen asleep again . .
Well, we'll have a bit uva chat and maybe then you'll wake
up, what? Jaysus this is a new one on me, a priest who
wants to go out for a cup of coffee before he'll hear your
confession! No, no, ya won't budge an inch from this or I'll
throw a fit! After all it's me statutory right to be confessed.

I pay me taxes! What do ya mean, taxes don't come into it!
If I'm not greatly mistaken we've a State Religion going
here and if I'm not greatly mistaken it's the State that pays
your wages .   . us taxpayers I mean: so I'm demanding me
State Religion hears me confession . . . no taxation without
confessionalisation! .   Come on with ya now Father, hear
me confession .   I've such a tide of faith washing over me
here, it's drowning me altogether . . . Pull yourself together
now Father and when we've finished, sure I'll stand you a
cup of coffee meself .   Yes . . . well, will we begin? All
right then, so. What?   . . The last time I made a
confession? I'll have to think about that for a minute, now.
Of course I'm a believer, why else would I be here at
confession? I'm a believing, practising, professing Catholic
    . the whole shebang   ! Twenty years .   . yes, the last
time I made a confession was exactly twenty years ago – the
day I got married .   . In church, of course . . . O the
service was gorgeous altogether! Well to tell you the God's
honest truth I didn't want a church wedding. I did it just to
keep his mother happy. She's a great believer. No, no I'm a
believer too, all right, only I'm a Socialist as well: a Socialist
believer! Not a theist, not an atheist, not antitheist . . . I'm
a Marxist, stroke Marxist-Leninist, Leninist, ptolomaic,
apostolic Socialist .   yes all right so, you'd be hard put to
call me a *great* believer: twenty years without making a
confession, I'll admit that looks bad. But I've always been a
great one for the self criticism . . . I did it nearly all the
time at me Union meetings and isn't that the same thing,
now? What's that? Will we begin? Yes, I'm ready. (*She gets
to her feet, with gravity.*) I solemnly swear to tell the truth,
the whole truth and nothing but .   .(*Suddenly interrupts
herself.*) What am I doing? Oh yes, I'm sorry, that's wrong,
Father, but ya know, I've been to that many trials . .
(*Makes herself comfortable on the steps of the confessional.*)
Oh I've been on trial times galore! (*Takes out her knitting
and begins to knit.*) Well now then, let's see . . . resisting
arrest . . . grand larceny . . . and it wasn't so grand, was it,
since I let myself get nabbed! Clueless larceny's more like
it! Sorry? No I am not a habitual thief . . . Only every now

and again . . . just for gas . . . no no, that was just my little
joke, I was only coddin' . . . There was one little game I
started off . . I called it 'housewives' discount' – that's
great crack . . . I used to organise a whole gang of women –
thirty or forty or fifty of us – from round and about and
we'd go off to the supermarket for the messages . .   'How
much is this sack of potatoes?' 'Three punts' 'Well we're
offering you one fifty . . . that's a housewives' discount of
fifty per cent, and that still leaves you a fifty per cent
profit . . .' Great crack, don't you think, Father? (*She's
amazed*.) . . . It's a sin, Father? A mortal sin? And what's
inflation, if it's not a mortal sin? Well I did it anyway .
You'd better keep a running total of all me sins and then ya
can tot up the penance at the end . . . Of course I've a
family . . A husband and a son . . . no they don't steal
     No I don't live at home .   well, wherever I can, really
. here and there .   . Oh, I know, I know   . as a wife
and a mother I'm not exactly a model of virtue . . . well to
tell you the God's honest truth..   . if I've turned into this
dirty trollop you see here .   . it's just because up till this
very minute, I used to go beyond the beyond as a model of
virtue. I'd have given me son the last drop of blood in me
body. I even packed in me job for him . . . so's I could be
near him and keep an eye on him personally . . . and it was
a job I liked and all .   . I was a shop steward I was .   . I
watched over him like he was the Infant Jaysus Himself
And I .   . well I felt like I was the Holy Virgin .   and as
for the oul fella . . . well he was St Joseph, the ox and the
blessed ass all rolled into one! Then the son grew up and he
went to school and he got mixed up in those bloody politics
     When he got to senior school, they were all getting
involved in protests .   . you know, all the clashes with the
polis .   . United Ireland and all that carry on .   . One time
he came home to me, God he was massacred . . . blood
from head to toe .   I passed out with the fright, Father, I
passed out! And from that day on, whenever he was a
minute late, or if I heard an ambulance siren going, I'd start
shouting: 'It's me son! It's me son!' Father, Father, you've
no idea what it's like to be a mother, Father! Mother of a

provisional republican extremist! And then at home, the chiseler would be arguing with me and the oul fella morning noon and night . . . and you know me and him, we're both practising Irish Labour Party believers! He used to call us every name under the sun! The nicest things he could find to call us were: 'Social democrats, liberal incense swingers!' God that used to really stick in me craw. O God that used to make me spit . . . He was going up me nose, d'you see? (*Raising her voice.*) 'And where the merry hell are ya off to now?' . No, no Father, I'm not giving out to you . . . I'd hardly say 'merry hell' to you, would I? Really, I hardly even know ya . . . I used to say to me son:

'And where the merry hell are ya off to now?'
'I'm going out with the fellow patriots.'
'And why? Aren't your Da and I your fellow patriots?'
'No, you're the FAMILY!!'

And he'd spit the word 'family' at me like he was hurling a bucket of shi – i – . . . mmm . . . (*She suddenly stops and corrects herself.*) potting compost . at me.

'No, no . . . yous, yous . Yez aren't fellow patriots', he'd say, 'Yez are just hooligans . . gets . . greasers crawling up the Brits' arses, that what yez are!'

That's the sort of thing he'd say to me and the Da, d'ya see, Father? You know, Father it got to the stage where I'd start going on Sinn Fein demonstrations meself! Well, I couldn't just sit on me backside in the house waiting for them to bring him home in a coffin, could I? . . . I'd get into the march, ten paces behind him so I could keep a sharp eye on him without being spotted. The worst of it was I had to shout the same slogans they were shouting so's I wouldn't stick out in the crowd. As long as it was stuff against the Brits that was fine . . but when they started on things I believed in . . . screaming death to the Labour party and such like at the top of my voice . . Oh Jaysus, Jaysus Mary and Joseph, I felt sick to the stomach, Father . . . And then there was all the marching and the running . . (*She gets up and walks about as if she's on a demonstration . . . passes to*

the left of the confessional.) And every time .   . (*She*
realises the priest still thinks she's on the other side of the
confessional, so she knocks on the grille.) Father, I'm over
here, Father .   . (*Sits down.*) No I don't feel bad for going
on the marches Father . . . it's just that every time I'd be
shouting me head off with one of these slogans, wouldn't I
find meself staring into the eyes of someone from me
Labour Party branch .   . maybe even the Secretary,
standing there on the pavement .   . and hearing me coming
out with all that stuff .   . and then they'd give me a sort of
old fashioned look .   . And in the end they threw me out of
the Labour party, because I was an embarrassment .   .
And all because I loved me son. Oh God, Love has really
banjaxed me Father   . . It's really banjaxed me! You take
a tip from me Father, don't you ever go and fall in love .
Listen to this one, Father   . . There was a march one time,
and I'd asked beforehand, 'What sort of march is it
tomorrow, Fellow Patriots?'

'Peaceful.'

So I gets meself all done up like a dog's dinner for a
peaceful demonstration: a pair of shoes with heels this high.
(*She mimes the height of the heels with her hand.*) A narrow
little pencil skirt .   .Well there was a polis charge . . .
you'd seen nothing like it in a month of Sundays! We had
the whole crowd of them up our backsides: Gardai, polis
dogs .   . Jesus, I even had the mounted polis and the
Customs and Excise after me! And me tearing off like an
eejit on heels as high as Nelson's Pillar – if I'd fallen off
them I'd've broken every bone in me body .   . and the skirt
pulled up to here so's I could run faster . . . and every
polisman in creation after me! And there's me, shouting
'What the hell do yez want? Feck off out of this!!' Holy
Mother, what a race .   . all the way down O'Connell
Street, up Grafton Street and round Stephen's Green . . . I
must have done the marathon, going like a bat out of hell! I
was wrecked – sweating like a pig, the heart was lepping out
of me .   . I was ruined altogether! I had soft boiled ovaries!

.   . (*Evidently the priest is reproaching her.*) Oh yes, I
know, 'That's not a nice thing to say . . . that's not a nice
thing to say .   .' I'd like to see you Father .   . Have you
ever tried running in high heels? (*Carries on with her story.*)
Clouds of smoke! Rubber bullets! Tear gas! Incendiary
devices! Molotov cocktails! And there was me   . I'd lost
the son .   . and I was shouting 'Son, son, where are ya
son?'   . And every other son of every other mother was
shouting back 'I'm over here!' And then all of a sudden,
didn't I catch a glimpse of the lad on the other side of the
street in the hands of a polisman who's belting him round
his little white face-een 'Whack, whack   ' Well that was
it, I let out a scream like a banshee! I ran across the road
.   . never mind the smoke bombs whizzing past at head
height – and a woman's head height at that! I grabbed the
polisman by the helmet and sank me teeth into his ear . .
and if his palsers hadn't arrived to drag me off . . . well I
won't tell you a lie   I'd have eaten him whole!

I shouldn't carry on like that? But listen to me Father, he's
me son. I made him .   . I put nine months of hard work
into making him: two eyes, ten fingers, ten toes, all his
teeth – and that bloody polisman was going to ruin all my
hard work in five minutes! So the son managed to get away
.   . Not me! They kicked the shite out of me and then
threw me into prison. Then I was put on trial. It went on
and on it was endless   . and Jaysus, Father they went on
and on about that bloody ear! . . . And it wasn't anything to
write home about after all .   . The judge gave out to me in
this tremendious voice: 'You have attacked the ear of the
State!' What I went through! And all for love of the son!
Oh God, like I said, love has really banjaxed me, Father!

Now me marriage . . . that was a love match all right. (*She's
inspired.*) O God, Father, I loved that husband of mine .
(*Change of tone.*) before I married him . . . No, no
afterwards as well . . . but afterwards, when we'd set up
house and started to have our first raging shindigs . . . (*She
stops suddenly and tries to finds another word.*) ideological
disputations . . . well you see I didn't hold with the

husband's ideological-social-political-housekeeping. Well I worked eight hours a day just like him, only there was one great difference: when I got home I had to go on working the other eighty hours of the week as well: washing, ironing, cooking, making the beds. Himself? Oh no! In the door, straight into the armchair and wham! (*Mimes turning on the television.*) Children's television! Bill and Ben the Flowerpot Men!!

'Well I'm not standing for this: I'm out all day, working like a slaveen', sez I, 'I'm as shagged out as you are . . Who ever said that Women's Liberation began and ended with a full time job? Well, look at me . . I've a full time job . but what about all this other work, the housework? Who gets stuck with that? I'm the bloody eejit who gets stuck with it! And who's paying me the wages for this job? Divil damn the one!! Queer sort of Women's Liberation I must say: get married and find yourself doing two full time jobs!' And anyway the husband suffers from the asthma . . nervous asthma   And when I'd got to the end of me tether .   well, you know what I mean, Father   . I just couldn't take any more . . 'I've had it up to here' I shouted, 'I'm packin me bags'   . and aarrrgh . .   that brings on an attack . . (*Imitates the panting of an asthmatic.*) Hurhh, hurhh, hurhh . . . flat out like a kippered herrin'   . couldn't get a breath at all. Aaaah!
   Put the heart crossways in me! 'No, no, darling, I didn't mean it! I won't leave you, I won't leave you! I'll stay with you for ever and ever!' So he gradually calmed down and the attack passed off and there was I, up to me uxters in it again! And pregnant into the bargain! . . Oh no Father, I didn't think it was a disaster . . I wanted this kid! He was part of the five year plan! I was thrilled to be up the pole . it was the real Alla Daley!! Nine months of gawking me guts up! In bed the whole time for fear of losing it! And in between vomiting attacks, I'd talk to meself in a passion of holy ecstasy: 'This kid is going to transform me whole life,' I'd say to meself, 'What is a woman if she's not a mother? She's nothing! She's just a being of the female

gender!' . . . What a fuckin eejit I was! . . . Oh, sorry,
Father, I meant what an awful gobshi-i . . . oh well, you
know what I mean, Father . . . ! Yes, now I'm getting on to
the sins . . . but don't ya see, if I don't give ya the run up to
them then ya might get the wrong end of the stick . .   Well
all right if ya say so, I'll skip over all that, and get to two
years ago . . . Well, two years ago I discovered me son was
inta drugs! How the hell should I know if they were hard
drugs or soft drugs .   I just heard the word 'drugs', and
that was it, I was off .   'He's a deviant . . . a dropout
a monster . . . !' I'm screaming, tearing me hair out,
'Where did I go wrong?', I asked meself, and then I asked
the oul fella, 'Where did you go wrong?' And all he could
say was 'Hurrhh, hurrhh .   .' (*She repeats the asthmatic
panting.*) And the son and all his shaggin' pals weren't very
impressed with me reaction: 'Oh for the love of Mike will
ya give over . . heroin's one thing, that stuff can kill ya,
but a joint every now and then, that's a different story
altogether   .' And there's me, wagging me finger at him,
'I'm not as green as I'm cabbage lookin', that's a load of
bollix . . . drug-taking is an ideological act and if ya don't
give up this minute, I'll throw ya out into the street . . . you
and all those feckin' pals of yours .   . and your little hoors
as well .   .' Sez he, 'What did ya say??!! That's a gross
insult! I'm packing me bags .   .!' 'Where are ya off to, you
little sparrowfart', sez I, 'Round to your Granny's!?' 'No,
I'm leaving!' So I stick to me guns – I wasn't just talking for
the sake of hearing me belly rattle – 'Well, clear off, then, I
don't give a tinker's damn what ya think .   ' . . And the
heart is crossways in me   . bump, bump . . 'I'd like to
see how long ya'll stay away . . . I'll give ya three days .
at the most .   . and then we'll be seeing ya running home
to yer Ma   .   '

A week goes by. No sign of him. I couldn't eat, I couldn't
sleep . . . and the oul fella .   'Hurrhh, hurrhh .   .
hurrhh, hurrhh . . . ' (*She repeats the asthmatic panting.*) I
went looking for him .   . searched high and low .   . the sit-
ins, the squats .   . Not a soul would open their mouths to

me – well ya see, I was a mother! Archetypal symbol of
repression! Absolute bond of silence in the face of the
enemy! 'Aha! This lot won't utter a word to me because I'm
a mother, is that it? Well, I'll banjax them . . . I'll
malavogue the lot of them! I'll disguise myself . . .' As
what? As a hippy   Yes, a hippy, Father! What are
hippies? Well they're dropouts . . . spongers . . . layabouts
 . . the ones who have a great life! Yes I know I was a bit
old to be a hippy   'I'll be a tinker! Tinkers are ageless!' I
said to meself .   . so I went off to the Oxfam shop and
Cancer Relief and decked meself out . . . ya know the sort
of thing .   . real Indian sari silk manufactured in Bradford
– and I got meself done up like a dog's dinner . .   Tunisian
sandals . . . a long Moroccan skirt . . . embroidered Afghan
coat, a Palestinian scarf from the Sinn Fein bring-and-buy –
purple eyeshadow, a pink spot in the middle of the
forehead, a gold cap stuck over the front tooth here – it was
me sister's, it fell off her one time three years ago when she
sneezed – rings, glass, necklaces and hoops in the ears .

So I took meself off to a commune full of mixed hippies .
males and females . . . not to mention a few oul dossers
flung in to make up the numbers . . . I make me entrance
 . (*She paces majestically to the other side of the
confessional.*) .   . looking like a bloody Christmas tree! I
was tinkling from head to foot! (*She knocks on the grille.*)
  I'm over here Father!   . . Will ya for God's sake pay
attention! Now then, so . . . I make me entrance .   . for
God's sake, even a dead dog would've lifted its leg at the
sight of me! I take meself off on me own . . . go off into a
corner and get sat down . . . dump me stuff and pretend I'm
going to sleep . .   Then at the right moment I produce a
little bottle of hooch I'd mixed up with my own fair hand –
turps, cod liver oil, horse manure, a few shreds of roll-your-
own tobacco, surgical spirit, iodine . . . Harpic . . . a drop
of lemon juice, and a nice squeeze of Colgate to bind it all
together – and I start sniffing this concoction, with me eyes
going round like Catherine wheels – solid gone, man! In
three seconds flat, they're all in a circle round me. 'What

are you doing?' 'Doing drugs, man.' 'What is it?' 'Heavy,
man.' 'Give us a go, will you!' 'Well, be careful .   . I don't
want any deaths on my conscience . . .' And away they
went, poking my bottleen up their noses till I thought it was
going to come out of the top of their heads . . . 'O man .
this is heavy stuff .   ' Ya see what a power of good
toothpaste can do ya – it can really blow your mind! Poor
kids . . . well of course they were all over me . . . 'Who are
you? Where do ya come from?' I was an interesting item all
of a sudden! O God, the tales I spun them, Father   'Me
Ma's a direct descendant of Pocahontas .   . an' the oul
fella's a tinker from Connemara . . . I earn a bite casting
spells and telling fortunes . . . and I live on chicken's blood
and freshly slaughtered cats because I'm a witch'   . No of
course they didn't believe me, but they were very nice and
let me stay with them .   Me son? Never saw hide nor light
of him .   Only once I caught a glimpse of him at a concert
in the Phoenix Park   'That bloody little gurrier,' I said
to meself, 'Now I'll get a hold of him' .   . So I'm trying to
push me way over to him, when you wouldn't believe it, all
hell suddenly breaks loose! All hell! They're running round
like chickens with no heads, setting fire to the loudspeakers
   . and the stage .   and the band . . . The polis wade in
   . Guess who gets nabbed straight off?   Right first
time! So when they put the handcuffs on me, I sez, 'Oh
there yez are! I was just beginning to get worried!' They
carted me off to prison so, but I was out again in a flash .
three days later   . because I had nothing to do with the
fire . . . So I come outside, and there's this great crowd of
people: hippies and Sinn Feiners and feminists all sorts .
they'd all come to meet me . .   They were waiting for me!
They'd made a banner . .   'Free the witch Mammy!' Such a
commotion, Father, a bloody great party! I'd no idea I'd so
many friends!   I hadn't done anything for them . . . they
just loved me . . for being meself . . . There was a little
girl right at the front holding out a chicken: 'Here's a nice
cup of coffee for you'   . sez she . . . So that's how I really
and truly began to live with these kids and I began to listen
to what they had to say for themselves .   At the start of

it, I didn't understand a word . . . and then I did begin to understand. They were saying, 'The personal is political . . explore your own sexuality!'   Yes, Father, sexuality! 'Rock against the rich! Power to the people! Power to enjoyment! Power to the imagination! Down with the capitalist work ethic!'

Sings in Gregorian chant.
'Work sets man free,
That's what they wrote
Upon the walls of the camp .
The Nazi camp   '

No? Gregorian chant isn't your cup of tay?
Make love not war!! (*Sings.*) 'If you're going to San
Francisco .   . be sure to wear   .'

Yes, Father, I'm calm .   . (*She kneels down.*) Yes I'm
listening . . . (*She repeats the priest's words.*) .   . I have
fallen into the abyss . . . the infernal abyss .   . moral
degeneracy .   . moral disorder . . . O I see what ya want
. . . order, is that it, Father? Order! *Orders! Rules!
Regulations!*

From the day I was born, my whole life long, I've had this
rigmarole drummed into me

One two, buckle your shoe,
Three four, close the door,
Five six, hands off your dicks,
Seven eight, don't be late,
Nine ten, do it again .

Stand up, sit down, be good, behave,
Your Mammy's your Mammy right into your grave.
Boys are boys and girls are dirt.
Hands off that thing that goes off with a squirt.

Slugs and snails and puppy dog's tails
Girls are girls and boys are males.
The boys stand up to do a wee,
The girls sit down, that's nicer, see.

But when they want to have a poo
They both sit down and so do you.
Everybody poos the same
But playing with poo's a naughty game
Don't touch the poo, don't touch the poo,
Poo poo's dirty, so are you

She is talking to an imaginary child sitting on her left.

Hands off the willy! Hands off the willy!
We don't play with the willy!! (*Her voice getting languid.*)
Little piss-pot   . (*She turns to an imaginary child on her
right .   . she's suddenly angry.*) Little wizened cow!!

Baby boys don't touch their willies,
Willies're dirty, just like poos .
Baby boys don't touch the girlies,
Girls are muck, poo and wee too!

Well now, do ya want to know what I think, Father? Now
pay attention, because I don't want ya to misunderstand me
. . . I've found something out . . . Love is disorder! Life,
liberty, fantasy .   . it's all disorder! .   . But you want to
impose order on us, Father   . making love just for the
love of it, Father . . . without that millstone of engagements
and dowries . . 'I'd like to introduce me parents . . .' It's
gorgeous making love for the love of it, Father! I tell ya it's
gorgeous! Well ya should try it before ya criticise! Father I
did it once with a boy and I don't even remember his name
 . I remember his eyes, his nose, his mouth .   . I
remember his hands and the things he said to me while we
were doing it .   . 'O God! .   . Mary, mother of God! .
O Sweet Jaysus! . . . O that's good! O God, I died and went
to Heaven!' .   . And him an atheist! I'm a lost soul? Well
now then, what would you say if I told you I'd found me
way? I'm not a lost soul, I'm a free spirit and it feels
terrific!! And I've absolutely no desire to go back, to go
home to me family . . . And that's what I told me son . .
Oh yes he came looking for me .   . He found me straight
off . . . Ya should have seen him: smart suit, neat as a pin,
short hair, tie. A right little toff he was .   'Mother I've

gone home! I got sick to the stomach of living like an
outlaw. I left Sinn Fein .   I've got my head together. I'm
not smoking dope any more . Even Father's got his act
together: he plays tennis, doesn't have asthma attacks any
more   . he's got a girlfriend, but if ya come home he'll
give her the boot. *Come Home Mother'.*

(*She mimes retching.*) O God, I felt like throwing up! Yes,
ya see, it all came to me in a blinding flash!   I could see
meself back home   with all that shite: shopping, ironing
shirts, never a moment to meself   ya know Father if I
ever wanted to read the newspaper   I had to lock meself
in the lav! So if I was ever constipated, I hadn't a clue what
was going on in the world! 'No, son .   I don't want
I'm not ready yet . . . ya see   ' 'You ought to be
ashamed of yourself! You're going round like an oul
dosser!'   'I know, ya're right .   . And I won't go around
like an oul dosser any more. I'll find meself some little job
   . part time will do .   . just to eat and keep a roof over
me head .   But I want to spend the rest of the time with
people   with women .   . I want to share what I've got
with them .   . I've a load of useful things inside me ya
know   and in return I'll take what they want to share
with me   their experiences . . . I want to talk .   . I want
to laugh . . . I want to sing .   I want to sit and look at the
sky   . Did ya ever know the sky was blue, me boy? I
never knew that! No pet, I'm not coming home, not even if
ya send a wagon load of polis to haul me back.'

And that's exactly what they did! Sent a wagon load of
Gardai to fetch me home!   Bad scrant to them .
that's what they did – me son and me husband laid a
complaint against me: desertion of the family domicile! And
to think, Father, the Gardai had the bloody nerve to follow
me right into the church .   what do ya mean, where are
they .   They're over there – near the sacristy – do ya not
see them? .   Father, what are ya doing? Father, don't call
them .   Have ya gone mad? . . Ya can't betray the
sanctity of the confessional .   . (*Runs to pick up her bag.*)
Ya couldn't do such a .   Shut yer bloody trap, will ya

(*She runs towards the exit.*) No . . . I don't want to go home with the Gardai! (*Mimes being seized by the policemen and handcuffed.*) O all right then .   . let's go . . . as I'm an adult over the age of consent . . . I'll decide what to do with me own life . . . (*She stops suddenly, turns towards the confessional and shouts.*) Spy! Spy! You're not a son of Mary!! Spy! Spy! You're not a son of Mary!!

Blackout.

Music.

translated by GILLIAN HANNA

The Same Old Story

A young woman stretched out on a rostrum. Dim light.

No, no, please . . . please . . keep still . . not like that, I
can't breathe. Wait . Yes of course I like making love,
but I'd like a bit more . well I don't know how to put it
. . you're squashing me flat . . Get off me . Stop that!
You're slobbering all over my face . No! No, not in my
ear! Yes, I like it OK but your tongue's going round like an
egg-beater! My God, how many hands have you got? Let
me breathe, will you? Christ you weigh a ton . What've
you been eating today? I said get o-o-ff me! (*She wiggles out
slowly as if freeing herself from the heavy weight of a man's
body and sits facing the audience.*) At last! I'm pouring with
sweat! You think that's supposed to be the way to make
love? Actually, yes, yes I do like making love, only I'd
rather do it with a bit of feeling . . . what do you mean I'm
being sentimental? There you go, I just knew you couldn't
resist that crack: I am not a romantic *Mills and Boon*-
reading cow! . I said I like making love, but I'm not a
bloody pin-ball machine . . . just slap 50p in the slot and all
the lights start flashing and zing, ting, zing . . . bang bang
wham!! And, if you feel like it, give it a bit of a whack! I am
not a pin-ball machine! If you give me a whack, my tilt light
comes on, get it? If a woman doesn't fall flat on her back,
skirt up, knickers down, legs wide open and willing the
minute you snap your fingers, she's a neurotic bitch; a
middle class prude carrying on like a vestal virgin all
because of her repressed reactionary-imperialist-capitalist-
masonic-Austro-Hungarian-church-ridden up-bringing!
Smart arse, aren't I? And smart arse women are just

ball-breakers, aren't they? You'd much rather have a bimbo with no brain and a sexy giggle. (*Imitates, low laugh, strangulated/sexy.*) Oh go away . . . why don't you leave me then? (*She hums nervously, then jumps in with.*) What am I talking about? You know I don't mean it . . . No, no . . I'm not upset . . . All right then, let's get on with the sodding love-making. (*She lies down again, in profile to the audience.*) It's not as if you don't know how to be gentle when you want to be . . . sometimes you're almost human . . . almost a comrade . . . (*She becomes languid, talks in a dreamy voice.*) I can say things to you I can't even begin to say to anyone else . . . intelligent things . . . that's it, you make me feel intelligent! I discover myself when I'm with you . . . and you don't go out with me just because I'm good in bed . . and afterwards you lie snuggled up close to me . . . and I talk and you listen . . . (*More and more languid.*) and you talk and I listen. You talk and talk and I . (*Extremely languid.*) and I . . . (*Just from her tone of voice we realise that she is about to have an orgasm.*) and I . . and I . . . (*Complete change of voice: she's wide awake and terrified.*) get pregnant.

(*Begging.*) Stop . . . stop. (*An order.*) Stop!! Christ, you're like a clockwork rabbit on a pogo stick! (*The man finally stops.*) I've got to tell you something very important . . . I'm not on the pill . . . No I stopped taking it . . . it makes me feel sick . . . makes my boobs swell up like the dome of St Paul's Cathedral.

Yes, it's OK, let's carry on . . . but for God's sake be careful . . . remember what happened that other time . . . God, I felt awful . . . (*Change of tone.*) Yes I know you felt awful too, but I felt worse than you, if you don't mind!

Yes, let's carry on, but be careful . . . (*They start making love again. She lies stock still, in silence for a while, she looks scared, she's tapping her foot nervously. She looks at her imaginary partner and whispers in a scared voice.*) Be careful! (*She's detached from what's going on, says in a stronger voice.*) Be careful!!! (*Annoyed.*) No I can't. I can't!

I'm so terrified of getting pregnant I've gone as stiff as a board! The cap? Yes I've got one, but you never said we were going to . anyway I don't like that rubber thing stuck up me . it makes me feel . . . like I've got a lump of old chewing gum inside me . . . (*The man pulls away from the woman. She sits up again facing the audience. She's not pleased.*) You've gone off the whole idea? Well, so sorry to inconvenience you! There is a funny side to all this though. I don't want to get pregnant and he's gone off the whole idea! (*She gradually gets more and more angry.*) And you're supposed to be a 'comrade'? Give me a break! Do you know what sort of comrade you are? You're a dick's comrade! Yessiree! That's what you think with! Your dick is your real true comrade! He's the repressed-church-ridden-plutocratic-masonic imperialist! Now I come to examine it, it's got a cardinal's hat on! And a general's stripes . . . and it's doing a bloody Heil Hitler salute! Yes, Heil Hitler!!! (*She's furious.*) Bastard! (*She's on the verge of tears.*) How dare you say such a thing to me . . . (*Weeping.*) I do not think with my bloody womb . . . too right I'm crying, you've hurt me, you've really hurt me! (*She lies down as if the man had pushed her with some force.*) What the hell? O great, I cry and you get turned on? Oh . . oh . . yes, yes . let's make love (*Very loving.*) Me too, me too . . . I love you too . . it's not your fault . it's society's fault . . it's egoism . . . (*Becomes more and more languid.*) and imperialism . the multinationals . . . nuclear energy . stop! What's so turning on about nuclear energy? (*Change of tone.*) Stop . . Stop!!! (*She goes limp, lifeless. She speaks in a flat voice.*) You didn't stop! (*Desperate.*) I'm pregnant . . . (*She pushes him away.*) I'm pregnant . (*Shouts.*) I'm pregnant!!!

Light change: from dim to very bright. The young woman sits with her back to where her partner was. She is now in the doctor's surgery. She is being questioned by a mid-wife.

Yes, yes I'm pregnant.
Nearly three months .
Yes, I've had a test .

Yes, nurse, I'll lie down. (*She does so.*) Could you do it
gently please? Yes, I know it doesn't hurt, I know it's only
an examination, but I'm nervous . . . Well I wasn't brought
up to deal with this sort of thing .

Yes I've already had an abortion . . . a while ago . .
without an anaesthetic . . . local or general, nothing . .
'wide awake and fully conscious' as they say . . . It was
ghastly . . . terrible pain! The worst thing, though, was the
way they treated me .   . as if I was just a whore. And I
wasn't even allowed to scream! 'Shut up' they said 'You
made a mistake, now you're paying for it!' (*Change of tone.
Makes a gesture with her fingers showing she paid in money
as well as pain.*) Too right I paid for it! This time I want a
proper abortion .   . (*She sits up.*) I don't want any pain,
just a knockout general anaesthetic! I want a good kip! I
don't want to feel anything at all . . . nothing at all! I don't
want to know anything about it . . . not even what day of
the week they're going to do the abortion .   . you can put
me to sleep the week before and then when you've got time
you can just quietly get on with .

(*Change of tone.*) Two hundred and fifty? Two hundred and
fifty?! Yes I know all about the Act, nurse. Thank God for
1967 and the Blessed David Steel. And don't talk to me
about the National Health Service. First the nearest hospital
can't help because the consultant gynaecologist objects on
grounds of conscience, and then you have to wait six
months for an appointment at the one that will do it, and
then the Thursday morning clinic's been cancelled because
the central heating boiler's broken down and they can't find
Isambard Kingdom Brunel to come and fix it, and when the
bed is finally booked and you turn up at the hospital when
the card tells you to, you find they closed the ward down
yesterday because of the cuts and even if you could've got
in, there wouldn't have been anything to eat because
they've privatised the cleaning services and the place is
crawling with cockroaches . . . Oh I know all about the
NHS . . . hang around waiting for the NHS and my baby'll
be born age twenty-four, unemployed with an emigration

visa to Australia in his hand! So I decided to go private.
Two hundred and fifty! Now I understand what the
gynaecologists are conscientiously objecting to. It's
probably the same consultant who wouldn't do it at the
hospital on grounds of conscience who's up to his elbows in
you here on grounds of lining his pockets. Two hundred and
fifty for every conscientious objection . . . and these guys
are becoming millionaires and we're financing them! They
must have solid gold speculums!

(*She gets up. She's decided.*) No, nurse, I'm not going to do
it . . . No it's not the money, I could borrow it . . . I just
can't go along with extortion. (*Change of tone. Thoughtful.*)
And anyway, I want to have a child sooner or later . . . now
we've got this far . . . I'm going to keep it. (*She has finally
made her decision.*) I'm going to fulfil myself . . . yes, I'm
going to fulfil myself! . . . (*She is ecstatic. At the top of her
voice.*) I'm going to fulfil myself!!! (*She jumps onto the
rostrum with her back to the audience. She shouts happily.*)
Motherhood! Motherhood!! Motherho-o-o-d!!! Third
month, fourth month, fifth month. (*She turns round to face
the audience.*) Your boobs are swelling up, your belly's
swelling up . . . Yo! Ante-natal exercise classes to ensure a
healthy pregnancy! One two three four! Bend! Two three
four! (*She does so.*) Pant like a dog! (*She does so.*) Heh,
heh, he-e-eh . . Stretch: one two three four. Pant like a
dog. (*She does so.*) Heh heh he-e-eh . . . harder. (*She
breathes faster.*) My head's going round . . I'm going to
pass out . . (*She faints for a couple of seconds.*) Oh Jesus I
feel sick . . Ooh! I can feel it moving! (*She turns round to
sit facing the audience.*) The creature moved! It feels like
wings fluttering inside me . . (*In ecstasy.*) Oh that's sweet
. . . it's so sweet! . . (*She changes tone.*) Sweet! Ice cream
. . ice cream . . I've got to have ice cream with hot fudge
sauce and spaghetti on top and anchovies and melon and
salami!! (*Professional tone as if she were the midwife who's
talking to her.*) Deep exhalation from the abdomen: ha-a-a-
rgh. Deeper: ha-a-a-a-argh! (*Urging her.*) Deeper . . (*She
suddenly stops. She slowly lies down in the middle of the*

rostrum, her head towards the audience.) It's coming, it's coming . . . Yes, nurse, I am lying flat . . . Yes, nurse I am relaxing . . . Yes, nurse, panting like a dog . . . Oh, oh . . . Yes I am pushing . . . Oh God it's agony! It's agony . . . Aaargh! Aargh! (*She screams in pain.*) I can't take any more of this . . . you've got to do something . . . Aaargh . . . aaargh . . . Where is he? Where is he? . . . Outside? What's he doing? (*Changes tone.*) He's chain smoking! (*She sits up, turning to face the audience.*) Poor soul!! He's nervous!! . . . He's tense!! It's a pity he couldn't have been tense a bit earlier, when he got me pregnant!! (*She speaks directly to the women in the audience.*) I don't know about you, but this pregnancy business really gets up my nose; the woman ALWAYS gets pregnant and the man NEVER does! I'm sick to the teeth of it! I protest! It's like a fixation with me . . . I even dream about it at night: I dreamed that my bloke was the one who had the boobs! Beautiful! Huge! Round! I wanted to have a bit of a feel but he says: 'Don't you touch my little titties! My mother wouldn't like it!' God knows what he thought he had there! And then he explained that he is a she, a she-man . . . a special kind of man . . . if they have sexual intercourse with a woman and they don't use a contraceptive, they get pregnant! (*Turns sideways as if her boyfriend were sitting beside her. Mimes touching his breast.*) Mmmn, mmmnn . . . you're beautiful . . . come on, why don't you lie down . . . (*She lies down as if the man were under her.*) Come on, take your clothes off, I want to talk to you . . . What's the matter? . . . You seem nervous . . . tense . . . You're not on the pill? Who cares? I love you just the same! It doesn't matter if you're not on the pill . . . if you get pregnant the National Health Service will take care of everything . . . otherwise you can go private, general anaesthetic, I'll pay for the lot . . . Or if you want to keep the baby then I'll marry you . . . (*Insistent.*) Oh come on, let's make love, let's make love, what does it matter if you get pregnant: a man only fulfils himself when he becomes a MOTHER! (*Shouting.*) Mother!! Mo-o-the-e-r!! (*She returns to the position she was in before: lying down.*) It's born! It's born! (*She sits up, looking straight into the auditorium. She is full of hope.*) Is it a boy? . . . (*Disappointed.*) No? . . . (*Gobsmacked.*) Well what is it then? (*She illustrates what she is saying with mimed actions. At this point she is the mid-wife.*) Smack on the baby's bottom to get it breathing: smack, smack. Wail! Aah, aah! Cut the umbilical chord: snip! Tie the knot! Into the bath of hot water: splash! . . . Cold water: Brrrr Brrrr! Onto the scales: barely six and a half pounds. (*She goes back to being the mother again. Now the baby is on her knee.*) Mamma's good little girlie! Good girl! Feed! . . . Injection! Vaccination. Another injection. Enema. Thrrpp . What a lovely big poo! Throw-up. Feed. (*She mimes sucking.*) Thssp, thssp. Baby food. Homogenised. Vitamins. Tum ti tum my darling. Come on sweetheart, laugh, laugh. No, don't cry. Have a little burp. Look at your toys . . . O pretty toys . . . ding ding ding . . . no, don't throw them on the floor. Look here's your cereal . . No, don't spit it out. No, the spoon doesn't live on the floor! Yummy scrummy cereal! Don't throw it up. Bad girl! Grow up, come on, Mummy's beautiful girl, grow up! Now sit down here, (*She mimes putting the child sitting on her right.*) and I'll tell you a lovely fairy story . . . (*Throughout the telling of the story, she moves around and changes her voice to match the character she's playing.*) Now then . . . once upon a time there was a dear sweet little girl who had a beautiful dolly. Well, to tell you the truth the dolly wasn't beautiful at all; she was filthy dirty, she'd lost all her hair, and she was made of old rags. What's more, this dolly used the most terrible bad swear words and the little girl learned every word and repeated them. 'Who on earth taught you those dreadful words?' her Mummy asked her. 'My dolly', replied the little girl.

'You're telling fibs! Horrid little boys taught them to you.' 'No, it's my dolly . . . come on, dolly, say some rude words to my Mummy!' And the dolly, who was very obedient and always did everything the little girl told her to, because she loved her very much, immediately came out with a whole string of the most awful filthy words: 'Fucking cow! Bitch!

Up yours, you slag! Arsehole! (*Chanting*.) Arse-hole, arsehole, arse-hole!!' Ooooh!! And the Mummy was so cross,
she had gone bright red. She snatches the dolly out of the
little girls's hands, flings the window open and .   . splat!
hurls her down into the field on top of a dung heap.
'Naughty Mummy, naughty Mummy,' says the little girl,
and runs out into the field, but just at that moment a big
bad red cat happens to be passing by, and he snatches up
the dolly in his teeth and carries her off into the woods .
Night falls . . . darkness . . . and the wood turns into a huge
forest. The little girl is only little .   and she's frightened
.   . 'Oh dear, oh dear.' After a long time she sees a teeny
tiny light far far off in the distance .   . and she goes on
towards the teeny tiny light .   What could it be? A little
dwarf standing on top of a giant toadstool doing wee-wees –
phosphorescent wee wee!

'O dwarf, little dwarf, have you seen a big bad red cat with
a rag doll that says naughty words in his mouth?'

'There he is' says the dwarf, and he spurts a huge stream of
luminous wee wee all over the big bad red cat, who falls
down, splat, stone dead! Because it's a well known fact, of
course, that dwarf's wee wee is deadly poisonous to cats!

'Thank you, thank you!' the little girl starts shouting. The
dolly is absolutely soaked through with wee wee: 'Who the
fuck is this shitfaced bastard who's killed my big bad red
cat!? . . . I adored that cat .   . He used to beat me up,
shove me around, walk all over me, make me work like a
dog, do horrible things to me, but I loved him just the
same! He turned me into a slave, he made me cry, he made
me feel awful, that only made me love him more, because
after all he made me feel like a woman, and I had my
MAN! And now what am I going to do without my big bad
cat . . . you fucking bastard . . . shitface   . arsehole!
Dwarfy arsehole! Dwarfy .   . arsehole   . Dwarfy .
arsehole!!'

'Oh I'm just crazy about this foul mouthed dolly!' screams
the dwarf 'I could almost see myself marrying her!'

'No, I'm going to marry her!' And a terrible voice echoes from the deep dark of the wood, no longer lit up by the dwarf's luminous wee wee . . . Who could it possibly be? O horrors!! A terrifying wolf with huge teeth as big as tombstones!

'I'm going to marry her!'

'I don't like him' says the dolly, 'I don't like that dickhead wolf!'

'I am not a dickhead! I'm a computer programmer. A wicked witch cast a spell on me and transformed me into a wolf . . you can see I'm telling the truth because I've still got my mouse in my pocket . . . But if this delightful young virgin will kiss me on the forehead, I will straightaway turn back into a handsome young professional, easy reach of London, offering sincere and affectionate friendship!' The dolly gives the wolf a kiss and . . whoosh! out leaps an unbelievably handsome computer programmer!! . . . and he's so happy he lets fly an enormous fart right in the dwarf's face, and the dwarf falls down, stone dead! Because it's a well known fact that computer programmer's farts are deadly poisonous to dwarfs. As soon as she sets eyes on him, the little girl falls madly in love.

'Oh he's so handsome, he's so handsome!'
And the computer programmer . . . well you see, a long time had gone by and the little girl had grown up quite a bit . and she'd sprouted those round things that women have at the front . . and those other round bits at the back as well . . . and computer programmers go crazy about those kinds of round things . . . actually it's one of the optional courses they can study for their degree!

'I've changed my mind,' he says 'I'm not going to marry the dolly after all, I'm going to marry the little girl with the bouncing titties and the peachy bum!'

No sooner said than done! They got married and lived happily ever, ever after. The very next day . . . the dolly: 'Everybody out! I'm calling a meeting! Meeting! My dear

newly-wed shitheads! Enough of this happy ever, ever after!
I can't fucking st 1 it! You spend all day slobbering and
bonking each other stupid and no one takes any sodding
notice of me! And then he goes off to do his computing,
and you, young bride with the peachy bum, you sit here
twiddling your thumbs till he comes home in the evening
. . then he throws you straight onto the bed and it's bonk
bonk bonk again! You set the alarm two hours early in the
morning so there's time for more bonk bonk bonk   . and
after meals it's bonk bonk bonk again, and everyone knows
that's very bad for the digestion!' 'But I'm so happy', says
the little woman wifey, who already had a bun in the oven,
'I'm so much in love!' 'That's a load of balls!' replied the
rag dolly, 'You're talking through your arse . .   "I'm so
happy" indeed! . . I've never clapped eyes on a more
miserable fucking cow than you are . . . as much of a
miserable fucking cow as I was when I was shacked up with
the big bad red cat . . . but with the cat, however bad he
was, I could at least have a decent political argy-bargy
what on earth do you find to talk about?' 'Listen here, you
scumbag rag doll,' shouted the handsome young
professional offering sincere and affectionate friendship,
'Either you shut your face and stop winding my wife up or
I'll stick you head first down the bog!' And the rude dolly
says: 'Bog off yourself! Go take a flying fuck!'

She said that to the computer programmer! 'All right then, I
will bog off . . . but I'm going to take you with me, to wipe
my arse on!' No sooner said than done. The computer
programmer picks up the rag doll, goes to the lavatory and
locks himself in. 'No no! Please don't do it, my darling
husband! Please don't do such an awful thing to my dolly!
. . Open the door!' 'No I won't open the door! I'm sitting
here with my Y-fronts round my knees and now I'm going
to wipe my arse!!' Just then, he let out a terrible scream:
'Aaaargh!' A computerised scream! What on earth could
have happened? What had happened was that while he was
wiping his bottom . . . WHOOSH! . . . the dolly had
whizzed right up inside him, head first . . . and all there was

to be seen of her now was her little feet sticking out. 'Oh, help me, my wifey darling, an appalling thing has happened! The horrible dolly has gone right up my bottom . . . pull her out for me!' 'I'm pulling, I'm pulling, but she isn't budging . . .' 'Pull harder!' . . . 'She won't budge!' . 'Aaargh! It hurts like hell! I think I'm going to die . . . it feels like I'm having a baby! Help me wifey . . . quick, call the midwife!' The wifey does as she's told and goes to fetch the midwife. But just as she's opening the front door – as everyone knows the ways of the Lord are infinite and various – who should be passing by but a midwife! And on her apron was written, 'MIDWIFE' . . . All in back to front writing, to match the ambulances! 'Oh, Mrs Midwife! You're like manna from heaven! Please do sit down . . . A terrible thing has happened to my family . . .' When the midwife found herself face to face, as it were, with the computer programmer's huge bottom, and saw the dolly's feet sticking out, she said 'Well, thank goodness you remembered to put the slippers on! Is this your husband?' 'Yes .   ' 'It's going to be a difficult birth! It's in the breech position, feet first!' And then she burst out laughing! She laughed and laughed! . . . And you know what happens to women . . . (*To the audience.*) . . . you too . . . when they get a fit of giggles .   . (*She shouts.*) 'Wee wee! I'm wetting myself . . I may be a midwife, but someone's cast a spell on me . . . I'm peeing everywhere. Help! I don't want to cause a disaster .   . floods . . . I don't want anyone to die . . . I don't want anyone to die! .   . fetch me a bucket!' So they fetched her a bucket, and she weed into that in a most dignified manner, looking away into the far distance, like men do when they pee outside in the open air .   . and when she had finished, she said 'It's enchanted pee, give it to your husband to drink. It will make him evacuate his bowels.' The computer programmer says: 'What's going on, have we all gone completely barking in this house? You expect me to drink this midwife's pee? I don't even know the woman!'

'Allow me to introduce you . . .'

'No! I don't want to know her!'

'But, my love, you must evacuate your bowels!'

'Yes you've got a point . . . well let's jazz it up with a bit of vermouth, a squirt of angostura, a slosh of gin and a couple of drops of lemon juice . . . mmmn, that's good . . . I'm telling you that's really good! Want a taste?' 'No, no, you drink it all down . . .' And he drinks and he drinks . . and his stomach gets bigger and bigger . . and he drinks . . and it gets bigger . . . And Boom! . . He explodes! And there's nothing left of the computer programmer, not even the tiniest scrap of skin this small, not even the mouse he loved so much! But there is the dolly, all in one piece and laughing her head off. 'Did you see that!' she says to her friend, the grown-up little girl, 'You fucking stupid cow! I've freed you from the computer programmer! Now you are in control of your own body, you can make your own choices, you're *freeee*! Let's go!' The grown-up little girl picks up her dolly and hugs her tight and tight. And little by little the dolly vanishes into her heart – right inside! Now the grown-up little girl is all alone on a long long road . . And she walks and she walks till she comes to a huge tree. And under the tree are lots and lots of grown-up little girls just like her, and they're having a huge party: 'Sit down here beside us. We're all telling each other the story of our lives. You can begin . . ', they were saying to a little fair haired girl who was there. And the little fair haired girl began: 'When I was very small I had a rag dolly who used to say the most terrible dirty words.' 'So did I' . 'So did I'

'So did I' . . and all the little girls burst out laughing together, in chorus. And one of them says: 'No one would ever believe this! We've all got the same story . . . every single one of us . . exactly the same story to tell'.

translated by GILLIAN HANNA

Medea

'Come over here! Hurry up! Move yourself! Medea's locked
herself in the house with the two kids! She's ranting like
someone possessed! She's screaming her head off! She's
gone out of her mind! She won't listen to reason! Her eyes
are bulging out of her head – as though she'd been bitten by
a tarantula! She's gone mad with jealousy . . . she can't
believe it .   . her old man Jason's gone off with a younger
woman. She's got to get out of the house and leave the kids
– but she just won't face up to it. Medea just won't see
sense! You talk to her. You're the oldest, you know her
best .   . stop her being so stupid!'

'OK, I'm the oldest, I'll talk to her . . . I know her   . I'll
talk some sense into her .   . Medea! Medea! Come to the
door! I've got to talk to you. Listen to me, girl, have a bit of
sense, will you. Stop being so selfish. You should be
thinking about your kids. If Jason marries again, they'll be
much better off: bigger house to live in, nicer clothes to
wear, there'll always be masses of food on the table: they'll
be living in the lap of luxury . . . And they'll be going up in
the world . . . all the nobs and big wheels'll be bowing and
scraping to them .   . they might even get to live in the
King's Palace! You love your kids, don't you Medea? Well
then, you've got to make a sacrifice for the sake of the
children! Be a good mother and not a hysterical woman!
Just face it – you've got to give in with good grace for the
sake of your own flesh and blood.

'No . . . no . . . no one's made you look like a fool .   . no
one's insulted you. Your husband hasn't got a bad word to
say about you . . . he says you're the best woman in the

world .   he says no one could have loved those children
more than you have . . or him, come to that   . he says
he'll always think fondly of you

'What are you up to, Medea? Speak to me! Say something,
for God's sake. Open the door, Medea. Come out and talk
to us .   . we're all in the same boat as you .   we've been
through it too   . cried our eyes out! You're not the only
one who's been dumped by a husband – it's happened to us
too   we know what you're going through.

'Get out of the way! Medea's decided to come out!   . .
Here she is! My God, she looks like a ghost! Her hands are
white . . she's as pale as a sheet .   . you'd think she
hadn't a drop of blood left in her body

'Hold her up .   . she's going to fall down .   . sit down
here, Medea

'Make some space, will you .   . let her breathe.

'We're listening.

'Shut up, will you .   . she wants to say something .
Medea's going to speak.

'She can't speak! All that screaming's made her lose her
voice! Give her a glass of water, she's parched. There,
that's it .   . Now, say what you want to say, Medea. Tell us
about it . . It'll make you feel better   . Get it off your
chest .   . '

'Friends .   . my dear women friends .   . what does my
husband's new girlfriend look like? I've only seen her once,
and that was in the distance. I thought she looked .   . so
beautiful .   . so young .

'You know I was fresh and beautiful once   . when I was
sixteen and my husband first set eyes on me .   . I had long
black hair and white skin .   . and my breasts were so firm,
they used to practically burst out of my blouse .   . no
wrinkles on my neck .   . no sagging jowls .   . and my
stomach was so flat you couldn't even see it under my dress
    . my hips were so slender, my whole body was so fragile,

when he took me in his arms he was always petrified he was
going to snap me in two or hurt me . . . and when he made
love to me, his hands'd shake – he'd be shaking all over, he
was so terrified – even laying a finger on me seemed like
blasphemy to him.'

'We've all been through that, Medea. But it's over and
done with now. Gone . . it's just fate   women's
destiny: men trade us in for younger flesh, younger skin,
younger breasts, voices, lips . . it's the law of nature
that's how it's been since the world began!'

'What law are you talking about? Who dreamed up this
law? Did all you women think it up? Write it down? Did
you go out into the streets and get up on your soapbox and
bang your drum and say "This is the law! This is Holy
Writ!!"? It was men . . men . . men who dreamed it up
. they wrote it down, they signed and sealed it and said it
came down from Heaven on tablets of stone . . and then
the King gave it his seal of approval   and they did it to
use it against us – against women.'

'No Medea, it's the law of nature. It's natural. Men get
older slower than us. They ripen as they get older, we
wither . . we swell up and then we fade away . . . they get
wiser and more mature. We lose our power and they grow
more powerful   that's the rule that makes the world go
round.'

'What a bunch of idiots you are! Listen, I understand it all
so clearly now. Of all the clever things men have done to
get one over on us, this is the cleverest. They've got you
believing in their law . . they've brainwashed you . . . you
repeat the lessons they teach you like parrots and then you
think you're happy . . . you grovel at their feet and yet you
won't rebel!'

'Rebel? Listen, Medea, listen .   Talking like this is only
going to make the King angry . . Why do you have to set
yourself against his rule? Just calm down, Medea and ask
him to forgive you and then he'll leave you alone to live
your life in peace.'

'Live my life in peace? Live my life? What sort of life do you think I'll have? All alone? Shut up here in my house? Alone? Like a corpse? No voices . . . no laughter . . . no love of any kind . . . no children, no husband . . . they're celebrating already – and they haven't even buried me yet! And I'm supposed to keep my mouth shut for the sake of the children? That's just blackmail . . downright bloody blackmail!

'Listen to me, my friends . . The most awful thought has just occurred to me . . . I can't seem to get it out of my head . . . it's pounding in my heart: I've got to kill my children. Oh sure, I know I'll always be remembered as a wicked mother, a woman who was driven out of her mind with jealousy . . . but it's better to be remembered as a wild animal than forgotten like a pet nanny goat! Milk her, clip her, then throw her out. Send her to market and sell her . . . she won't even make a single bleat in protest! I have to kill my sons.'

'Help! Get over here quickly! Medea's gone off her head. She's not talking like a mother! She's ranting on like an old streetwalker . . . someone's put a spell on her . . she's absolutely barking mad!'

'No sisters, I haven't gone mad . . . I've thought about it over and over again; and over and over again I've stamped the idea out of my brain . . I've bitten my hands, I've beaten my arms with stones till they bled . . . all to stop myself using them as weapons against my own children . At first I thought I'd commit suicide: I couldn't bear the thought of being thrown out of my own home, banished from the country – even though I'm a foreigner and don't really belong here – I couldn't stand the thought of being carted away like some poxy old whore . . . Oh I know everyone despises me now – even you my dear friends – I'm a burden. Everyone's embarrassed by a woman who's surplus to requirements . . . especially when she kicks up a fuss. Even my kids would rather forget about me. And then when I've gone, everyone'll forget I ever existed . . . I'll be

as invisible as if they'd never had a mother at all . . . As if
Medea had never been born . . never been loved .
never been taken into bed by a man, never been caressed,
kissed or made love to. Medea was dead before she was
born! And if that's true, if I'm dead already, if everyone has
killed and buried me, then I can't kill myself all over again,
can I? I want to live! But I can't live unless my children are
dead . . I've got to kill my own children . . . flesh of my
flesh . . blood of my blood . . life of my life   '

'Aargh! Run, you lot. Go and get some rope . . we'll have
to tie the poor thing up! She's completely demented .
she's possessed by some sort of devil – it's making her say
these terrible things!'

'Get away from me! You lay one finger on me and I'll stab
you straight in the guts with this pitchfork!'

'Run for it! Run! She's gone berserk! Run for it! Run!
Stop! Wait! Jason's coming . . her husband's coming .
Get out of the way. He'll know how to handle his woman
. let him through

'Look Medea. You can calm down now . . it's your
husband, Jason.'

'Oh Jason, it's too kind of you to leave your sweet little
bride, your delicious rosebud, just to come and see me! Oh
look at his open honest face coming towards me . . but
he's walking a bit hesitantly . he looks a bit put out

'Sit down . . no it's all right . . I was only pretending to
be crazy . . I was only joking . . I wanted to put the fear
of God into this lot. I just felt like seeing them all run
around, weeping and wailing, and then laughing, laughing
till the tears ran down their cheeks! I've got nothing else to
do to pass the time these days. It's OK I'm quite lucid now.
The thing is, I've been going over and over all this in my
mind, and I've finally come to a conclusion: I must have
been completely stupid to think I could keep you all to
myself . . for ever. I just saw red . . I was just being a
typical brainless jealous woman . . well you know what

women are like . . . weak and spiteful, quick tempered . . .
we burst into tears at the slightest excuse . . . Say that you
forgive me, Jason. I can't help it, it's just my own weak
nature . . You did the right thing, finding a new young
bride . . . new bed, nice clean sheets . . . and you'll have a
whole new set of relatives – all very important people – and
they'll be my relatives too, because your family will be my
family . . . That makes me happy . . . very happy . . . If
you'll forgive me, I'll make all the arrangements for the
wedding . . I'll get the marriage bed ready for you and
scatter the sheets with rose petals . . . I'll be better than a
mother to your young bride .   . I'll teach her everything
she needs to know about love . . . If that'll make you
happy!   . Now do you believe I've come to my senses?

'And to think I called you a traitor! A man isn't a traitor
simply because he swaps one woman for another . . . a
woman ought to be happy just being a mother. After all,
that's the best reward she can possibly have. I can't think
what got into me, saying this law men have made, that lets
you trade in one woman for another, was a kind of
blackmail! What was I thinking of when I said this cage
you've got us locked up in was an unholy insult? Whatever
put the thought into my head that you'd chained our
children round our necks like millstones to keep us in our
places – just like you chain a hard wooden yoke round a
cow's neck to force her to stand docilely while she's milked
and mounted . . That's how crazy I was, Jason, I actually
believed all that . . and I still do!! And I'm going to smash
this cage you've got me shut up in . . . I'm going to throw
off the unbearable weight of the yoke you've laid on my
neck . . . I'm going to shatter your filthy blackmail once and
for all!! You've used your laws to chain me to my children,
and condemned me to a living death.

'My friends, listen to me breathing . . . with one breath,
with one deep breath I could breathe in all the air in the
whole wide world.

'My little boys have got to die, Jason. They've got to die so

that you can be crushed to a pulp – you and all these
stinking laws you've invented. My friends, give me the
weapon .   . poor desperate Medea . . . plunge the knife
into your children's soft flesh .   . aaah, they're bleeding
     it's like sweet honey   they're bleeding . . . Oh my
heart, forget these children are the flesh of my flesh .
they're bleeding .   . Don't shudder when they scream:
"Mother   have mercy   Mother!"

'And a terrible howl will echo round the world: "Monster
     bitch .   unnatural, cruel mother   . she-devil!" And
through my tears I'll whisper: (*Almost under her breath.*)

'Die, die, so your blood and bones can give birth to a new
woman! (*At the top of her voice.*) Die! You must give birth
to a new w-o-o-ma-a-a-n!!'

*The last syllable turns into a musical note which dies as the
light fades.*

                    translated by GILLIAN HANNA

More Stories

The Dancing Mistress: On the Assembly Line (1968)
Michele Lu Lanzone (1969)
The Rape (1975)
Alice in Wonderless Land (1977)
The Whore in the Madhouse (1977)
Coming Home (1983)

The Dancing Mistress:
On the Assembly Line

SPEAKER: (*offstage voice*) Today rhythm and harmony are at the root of production specially in modern firms. As we have seen in Japan for some time, qualified dancing instructors have been called in to train and teach workers on the shop floor.

Enter the dance teacher. The stage is completely empty.

TEACHER: (*towards the wings*) Come on you three we chose yesterday.

Enter the young women workers, rather hesitantly, and line up downstage beside the teacher. They carry out the movements under her direction.

Come on darlings, please. It's no good putting you straight on the assembly line if you haven't learned the twenty-four simple precise movements you have to make, keeping exact time to the music. It's simple, not tiring; you'll find it's elegant even, and enjoyable . . . But you'll have to pay close attention! Our motto is 'Work with joy!' Let's imagine that the high conveyor belt passes along at this height, and the lower belt moves at this level. You'll find the screws spaced out ten centimetres apart on the higher belt; each one of you, with both hands, must pick up two of them and insert them, first one hand then the other, in the holes in this structure on the lower belt. Now let's try   . that's right, like that, slowly .   . don't go too fast .   . slowly does it   . good, well done!

That wasn't difficult, was it? . . . One, two . . . one, two . . Now listen carefully: you'll see a kind of metallic cigar moving along on the higher belt, which you must pick up in your teeth . . . like this . . . ahmm .   . watch

out it's coming .   . ahmm .   . well done! Now, without
stopping what you are doing with your hands, insert the
fuse into the hole in the other end of the piece which will
come along on your left at that precise moment. There'll
be two more fuses to thread on . . . ahmm .   . one
threaded . . . ahmm .   . two threaded .   . so now with
two sharp blows with your forehead you tap home the
fuses . . . ohpp! ohpp! .   . start again with the basic
movement . . . one, two . . . steady does it . . . you
mustn't get tired .   . Isn't it fun? Simplicity itself and
great fun! Now, the third movement: using your nostrils
pick up the two little washers which you will find arriving
on the lower belt .   . breathe in, come on breathe
quickly .   . go! .   . Well done. Now you will see some
thin copper wires attached to the washers .   . two little
tugs to straighten them out . . . and then you wrap them
around the sprockets on the left-hand engine section.
Three turns is all they need. Right, go .   . one, two,
three .   . that'll do.

Now you blow out through your nose to get the washers
out .   . go on blow out hard .   . well done! . . . Now
take your right hand off a moment and attach the wire to
the sprocket on the lower belt . . . now do this gently .
wind it round like this .   . gracefully, well done, my
darlings .   . two little caresses with the palm of your
hand to do up the nuts on your left .   . slowly .   . one,
two! That's enough . . . careful now . . . near your right
foot there's a pedal which drives the shearing machine
.   . be careful to pull back your hands, or else zac .   . a
quick blow .   . and trac .   . you'll cut off your fingers
and we'll have them all over the floor .   . the boss
doesn't want that! It makes such a mess! Off we go .   .
well done . . . that's perfect! Now you stop the drive belt
with a sharp blow with the right thigh on the left piston
.   . good .   . and now two blows with your hip on the
right-hand piston like when you do a saucy walk! Another
with your left . . . zam! Bend the knees .   . pelvis
forward .   . until the tummy touches the rubber sucker

on the drill handle . . . push it . . . there! Gyrate the
pelvis . . . yes, that's right, just like the belly dance .
great . . . again! Now pull back the pelvis with a jerk . .
strike the lever just behind with the buttocks (*Reacting to
the mystified air on the faces of the women.*) . . . yes, I
mean stick out your arse, and the cycle comes to an end
so a new one can begin. Come on stick it out!! Ohpp!

See how simple it is? And you've got the additional
advantage of toning up the pectorals and fighting the flab.
Goodness knows how many women would pay to be in
your position! Right now, off we go again: let's go over it
slowly, catch hold of the screws up there and screw on the
ones down here . . . one, two . . . here come the
sprockets . . careful, now with the teeth . . ahmm!
Screw on the left-hand one straight away . . ohpp!
Another one . . one . . op . . two butts with the
forehead . . go on . . . go on . . that's perfect! Ready
with the nostrils, put in the two washers . . op, op .
two pulls on the wires, straighten them out . . . wind
them on the left one . . three turns . . . op! Go on . .
Stop! Sniff! Two sniffs, take the wires in the right hand
gently does it . . ooone . . . wind it on . . . twooo . .
threee . . Now the palm of your left hand . . caress the
nut, opp! Ready for a quick blow . . on the shearing
machine pedal! Go on . . zam! Two thrusts with the
right hip on the piston, one on the left . . now that
wiggle! . . . one the wiggle! Two . . third wiggle, to the
left! Well done, excellent! Now forward with the pelvis
. . . belly button right on the sucker handle . turn it
(*She sings.*) la-la-la-la-lai-lalala . . . Right now, ready
with your bottom on the lever to finish the cycle . . go
. . Good girls! . No don't stop: let's start from the
beginning again . . come on, if you make no mistakes
you'll get taken on! One, two . . . one, two, hands on the
screws . . pick up the . . . with your teeth . . one, two
and left . . . one, two and right . . push them in . .
blow with the head . . . two, op, pop . . . ready with your
nose stuck out . . take the washer with your nostrils .

two movements to stretch them out, op, pop .   wind
the wires round the spool on the left .   . vrr, vrrr .   . oh,
that's great! Sniff sniff . . . on with the right .   . steady
 . . ooone, twooo. wind it on . . . twooo, threee, left
palm to caress the nut .   . op. Sharp blow on the
shearing pedal; zamm!   . that wiggle . . . Two on the
right .   . left! Great!   . On you go with the belly
button .   . trapan .   . trapan on with the dance .   . on
with the sensual eastern promise   . on .   . on, bottoms
at the ready   . stick it out   . perfect

*They continue with a frantic rhythm, while the voice from
the loud speaker says.*

SPEAKER: In the Siemens factory in Milan, the assembly
line workers achieve four thousand five hundred
movements in a single day, three thousand of which are
made with the hips to work the shearing machine pedal.
The violent blows to which the pelvis is subjected have
caused most of the women to suffer from gynaecological
and pelvic disorders; some have had to undergo
operations which have left them unable to have children.

translated by CHRISTOPHER CAIRNS

Michele Lu Lanzone

Michele Lu Lanzone, a Sicilian trade unionist, was killed by the Mafia in the 1930s. His story is told by his mother, from inside the mental hospital where she has been confined.

The various voices are all performed by the one actress. The characters are portrayed by changes of tone and gesture – always epic, never naturalistic.

The stage is bare, except for a stool, centre-stage, on which **MICHELE'S MOTHER** *sits.*

Enter a woman, of no definable age: **MICHELE'S MOTHER**. *She is holding a rag doll, the size of a five-year-old child. She sits on the stool. She combs the child's hair, and rocks him in her arms.*

* * *

BOY: (*singing*)
    Michele Lu Lanzone,
      Don't be a fool.
    Leave the water to
      Run where it must.
    Down the road, there's
      Trouble coming,
    But stay out
      Of the way.
    True, there's no water
      In your valley,
    But there's no fighting spirit
      Among the peasants.

MICHELE'S MOTHER: (*speaking*) Please, please, keep out of this . . . (*Singing.*) Or you're going to end up dead! (*Speaking, with a little laugh.*) Do you like that little song? It's nice, isn't it? They made it up for your dad – just for him! You know, your father was a really important person. When he walked down the road, all the peasants of the valley used to raise their hats to him. Not because they thought he was better than them – no! It was out of respect. Because your dad was the finest, bravest trade unionist in the whole valley.

THE CROWD: (*shouting from a distance*) Michele . Long live Michele! Here's health and a long life to you!

MICHELE'S MOTHER: A long life . . Michele, leave things be. They've already killed more than seventy trade unionists. Seventy of them, dead and buried . . all because they got too involved, Michele, all because they sided with the peasants too much.

MICHELE: No! Times have changed! These days the Mafia has to lie low. They're on the defensive. They're under pressure from the Government Inquiry that's been set up. Don't you see? We've already forced them to break up the big landowners' property and hand over the land.

CROWD: But what are we supposed to do with that land, when we haven't got water? Even melons won't grow. Parched, everything's parched. They might as well give us the sands of the Libyan desert, for all the good that it'll do us!

MICHELE: There will be water! There will be water! All we need is for the dam to be built. The plans have already been approved. The Region has already voted the funds. It's only a matter of another couple of months.

I'm going now. I'm going to Palermo. I'm going with the mayors of every village in this valley. If necessary, you'll come too, with your wives, with your children . . and we'll make our voices heard!

BOY: (*singing*)
Michele Lu Lanzone – he's a Union man!
But Michele, Michele,
You're making us dance the goat dance!

MICHELE'S MOTHER: Ha! 'Let's do it,' you say. 'We *shall* do it' 'It's as good as done' – you sound like Moses in the wilderness: 'Be patient!' . . Patience!! And in the meantime we still have to go down to the Piano dei Greci, to work for the landowners, slaving on their farms. And our women too. And all our land is good for is for burying our dead. And our children? We have to send our children to work in the mines, in the salt mine, the sulphur mine, where they end up hunchbacked and stunted in their prime.

DISTANT VOICE: (*shouting*) Michele, people are saying that the bosses have sent you here. Yes, that you're paid by them so as to keep us quiet with promises.

MICHELE: (*moving to the front of the stage*) Who says so? Who?! Come out in the open! Say it to my face . (*Shouting.*) Son of a bastard!

MICHELE'S MOTHER: (*speaking*) Don't get angry, Michele. Let it be. This isn't the job for you. It's hard to be a union leader – you have to be cut out for it, you have to be born to it, you have to know what you're doing.

CROWD: (*shouting*) Every family's going to get three bags of flour from the Government! It's election time. 'That'll keep them quiet for a bit.'

MICHELE: (*speaking*) No! No! This is precisely the moment when we must move. Now! It's time to go and make our presence felt . . (*Shouting.*) . . Now!

MICHELE'S MOTHER: Michele, leave things be. Michele, you'll end up destroying yourself.

MICHELE: But don't you understand that it's the bosses

that don't want to let us have the dam? It's them who are blocking everything . . because with a dam there, the whole valley would become green and fertile. We would have so much water that we could even wash our feet in it! And we could have fountains in our village squares, like they do in Palermo! You see? Then you could live the good life, farming your land. All of you. And you'd be earning for yourselves, living off your own land! And then, tell me, where would the bosses find labourers to work for them on starvation wages, like they have up till now? And what about the sulphur mine? And the salt mine? Do you think that we'd go and slave in the mines any more, getting sores all over our bodies, like lepers? No! They'd be forced to close! That's why. That's the reason they don't want you to have this dam, even if it means the whole of Sicily blowing sky-high, because whatever happens, they're determined to keep you poor . and starving.

MICHELE'S MOTHER: Michele, stop it. Keep quiet; don't step out of line, Michele – they'll kill you

MICHELE: No! We – *us!* – we're going to make Sicily rise up! It's time we stopped being frightened. We Sicilians are capable of killing to avenge dishonour . . . But I ask you, isn't this a dishonour? To be beggars? To be hungry? To be exploited? Let's go. Let's all go to Palermo. Let's go and grab those bastards by their miserable throats.

MICHELE'S MOTHER: Ah, you should have seen him, Cenzino . . your father, right at the front of the march, marching proud, like the Bold Rinaldo with his two swords! And right behind him came the peasants, some of them on mules, some of them on donkeys, with their banners and placards, shouting and singing. They were going to Palermo. They were like flowing lava from the volcano.

BOY: (*singing*)
    Palermo, Palermo .

Here we come   !

MICHELE'S MOTHER: But they never made it. The
police arrived, by the truckload. There were over a
thousand of them. The bosses were watching the scene
from their villas, with binoculars. They beat them,
Cenzino   . beat them, with their rifle butts. Your dad
was taken off to prison – broken arm and all. They
sentenced him to twelve months in jail.

Michele .   Michele .   Why are you doing all this?
Michele, leave things be. You're getting too involved.
What's the use? The peasants have always been under
bosses. They're resigned to it. Don't start stirring them
up. No – you'll see, the employers will make you pay for
it.

She goes and huddles at the back of the stage.

BOY and MICHELE'S MOTHER: (*singing*)
    Michele Lu Lanzone,
        Don't be a fool.
    Leave the water to
        Run where it must.

MICHELE'S MOTHER: Yes, but then your father came
out of prison. Yes he did. But he didn't give up, no! He's
stubborn, like a dog with a bone. Now he began spending
all his time studying old maps at the Land Registry. One
evening he came home, singing and shouting:

MICHELE: Look what I've found! An old map! Heaven
knows how old . . . from before the time of the
Bourbons, probably   . . Maybe even from the time of
the Arabs. Here – look! There's a spring marked here, at
the head of our valley. It was blocked by a rockfall.
Maybe   maybe it was a really big stream. Maybe it's
still there. All we have to do is unblock it, and open it
up

MICHELE'S MOTHER: Leave it be, Michele. Don't be a
fool. Don't get involved. If nobody's ever uncovered that
spring, there must be a reason for it. Forget it, Michele.

A couple of days later – it was a Sunday – all the peasants set off, with their picks and shovels. The workers from the mine were with them too. And their wives, carrying earth in baskets balanced on their heads. And our old people too – in fact a couple of them had a guitar and an accordion, and played and sang for us, and we worked, almost as if we were dancing.

BOY and MICHELE'S MOTHER: (*singing*)
    The time of the red berries will come . .
    And I want to kiss the girls' red mouths .

MICHELE'S MOTHER: All of a sudden – it wasn't even midday – a shout went up. They'd found it! The hole was there – they'd found the spring! It was blocked with fallen bricks, the same sort of bricks they used in the olden days. Cenzino, you should have seen it! Everyone dived in at once, and started trying to dig. But they had to take it in turns, because there was only room for one person at a time . .   We formed a human chain, to pass out the bricks. And we sang.

BOY: (*singing*)
    Hopla! Hopla! Toss me a kiss and go!
    The time of the red berries will come .
    And I want to kiss the girls' red mouths . .

MICHELE'S MOTHER: Water! Water! It's coming! It's beginning to flow! You should have seen it, Cenzino. A jet of water – incredible – like thirty fountains all rolled into one! And there they all were, men and women, like crazy, running under the water and getting themselves soaked to the skin! Everyone jumping about and laughing. Water! Water! How good it was to have water.

BOY: (*singing*)
    The time of the red berries will come . . .
    And I want to kiss the girls' red mouths . . .

MICHELE'S MOTHER: We were drunk with it, drunk with water!

CROWD: They can keep their dam. We don't need it any
more. This stream will be enough to water the whole
valley   . every bit of farmland, and the pastures too.
Our corn won't get parched any more. And who's going
to go and work in the mine, now? They can shut that
rathole now. It can close, for all we care!

MICHELE'S MOTHER: But the next day, some of the
women came up the road, crying. 'The spring has stopped
running. It's run dry already.' The peasants went running
to look. 'No, no   . something's blocked the hole.' They
started digging .   digging

They dug down, and they pulled out what was blocking it.
It was   . Michele .   your father. He'd been killed,
and they'd jammed him down there like a plug.

(*Desperate.*) Michele! Take care! You don't have to do all
this, Michele! The peasants are resigned to their lot .
they always have been. (*Shouting.*) Justice! Yes – I want
justice! In God's name, is there no justice? Yes, by God –
there was! They arrested them – the ones who'd killed my
son. They put them in handcuffs and sent them for trial.
Twice! And twice they found them not guilty and set
them free. All of them. And the poor devils who knew
who had done it, and who went to give evidence at the
trial, they too were found dead, killed, with their tongues
cut out. (*Desperate.*) Michele   Leave things be,
Michele   We must have patience   . patience! (*With
a terrible anger.*) Patience! Wait till the lava flows. Yes –
the red lava of the volcano, that will burn everything in
its path – everything – the bosses, those who defend
them, those who protect them, everything! Everything
must burn – everything!

The lava .   here it comes! It's red. It's burning. Run,
run! No – you can't escape. Pigs, you filthy pigs! *Now* go
and call on the law to protect you! *Now* go and call your
judges, to defend you! (*Shouting.*) Pigs! You're all going
to burn! Pigs!

Michele – we've won! Michele .   . Michele .   .

BOY: (*singing*)
>Michele Lu Lanzone –
>>Don't be a fool.
>Leave the water to
>>Run where it must.
>Down the road, there's
>>Trouble coming
>But stay
>>Out of the way!

translated by ED EMERY

The Rape

There's a radio playing. But I only notice it after a while.

It takes me a while to realise it's someone singing.

Yes, it's a radio. Romantic music: love   . heart   . moon   . June . croon   . love

There's a knee, one knee, rammed into my spine .   the person behind me must be kneeling on the other one . Someone's gripping my hands with theirs. Strong hands . . Pulling my arms in opposite directions .   Twisting my left arm hardest

I don't know why, I find myself wondering if he's left-handed.

I don't understand anything that's happening to me.

I'm terrified   scared witless   . can't make a sound can't utter a word.

Everything filters into my brain slowly   incredibly slowly

Jesus . . . this is Bedlam . . . everything's so mixed up . How did I get into the back of this van? Did they give me a shove and then watch me clamber in, or did they lift me pick me up bodily

I don't know.
It's my heart knocking against my ribs, that's what's stopping me thinking straight . . . that and the pain in my left hand .   it's getting really unbearable now.

Why are they wrenching it so hard?
I'm not moving a muscle.

An iceberg.
Now the one behind me has taken his knee out of my back
. . . he's found a more comfortable position . . . he's got
himself sat down and he's holding me between his legs . . .
that's the way they used to hold kids when they took their
tonsils out in the old days.

That's the picture that floats into my brain.
Why are they squeezing me so hard?
I'm not moving .   . I'm not screaming .   . I can't scream.
I've lost my voice . . .

I don't understand what's happening to me at all.
They're still singing on the radio but it's not so loud.
What's the music for? Why have they turned it down now?
Maybe because I'm not screaming.
There are three others .   . besides the one who's holding
me.
I look at them .   . there isn't much light .   . not much
room either

Maybe that's why they haven't stretched me out flat
I have the feeling they're very calm. Very sure of
themselves.

What are they doing? Lighting a cigarette.
What the hell is going on? They're smoking? At a time like
this?

Why are they holding me like this and smoking at the same
time?

Something's going to happen. I can feel it . . . I take a deep
breath . . . two . . . three . . . No it doesn't help. Doesn't
clear my mind. I don't understand . . .

I'm simply terrified . . .
Now one of them's coming closer . . . another one sits down
on my right and one more on my left. I can see the red tips
of their cigarettes.

They're breathing heavily . . they're very close.
Yes . . something's going to happen . . I can sense it
The one behind me tenses his muscles .   I can feel them
    round my body.

He's not holding me any tighter, he's just tensed his muscles
    . like he wants to be ready to hold me tighter.

The one who moved first gets himself between my legs
he's on his knees .   . he pushes my legs apart.

It's a very precise movement and he seems to be working in
tandem with the one behind me because *he* immediately
clamps his feet over my parted legs, to keep them spread
wide open

I've got trousers on. Why are they spreading my legs when
I've still got my trousers on? This is worse than if I was
stark naked!

I'm distracted from thinking about this by a sensation I
can't quite identify   a sensation of heat on my left breast
    . it's slight at first .   then more intense .   . till it's
unbearable

A burn.

The cigarettes .   through the sweater, right through to the
skin.

I find myself wondering what you're supposed to do in this
situation – I can't do anything at all .   . can't speak .
can't cry

It's as if I'm outside myself .   . I'm outside a window being
forced to watch something appalling happening on the other
side of the glass.

The one squatting on my right lights the cigarettes, takes a
couple of drags and then passes them to the one between
my legs.

They smoke them fast. The stink of the scorching wool must
have unsettled them

They slit the front of my sweater open with a razor blade. They cut through my bra as well . . . and there's a shallow gash in my skin . . . later, expert medical opinion will measure the slash at eight and a half inches . . .

The one kneeling between my legs grabs my breasts in his open hands . . . they feel icy under the burns . .

Now they're undoing the zip of my trousers . . . and they all start undressing me; but they only take off one shoe, one trouser leg. The one holding me on the right is getting excited .   . I can feel his erection as he rubs himself against me.

Now the one between my legs is inside me.
I think I'm going to be sick. I must stay calm. Must stay calm.

'Move your hips, whore .   . show me a good time.'
I concentrate hard on the words of the songs . . . my heart is going to explode .   . I want to drown in the chaos inside my head . . . I don't want to understand what's going on . . . I don't understand words .   . I don't understand any language.

Another cigarette.

'Move your hips, whore.'

I've turned to stone.

Now another one's inside me. He's thrusting harder than the first one. It hurts like hell.
'Move your hips, whore!'

The blade they used to slit my sweater open is waved in front of my face a couple of times. I can't tell whether they've slashed me or not . . .

'Move your hips . . . whore . . . you're supposed to be showing me a good time!'

Blood's trickling down my cheeks into my ears.
Now it's the third one.

It's disgusting to feel a man inside you like this . . .
enjoying himself like a grunting wild beast . . .

'I'm dying . . .' I manage to stammer out . .   'I'm having a
heart attack.'

They believe me .   they don't believe me .   They
quarrel.
'Let's get her out. No!   Yes! .   ' Someone hits
someone . .
They stub a cigarette out on my neck .   . here.
It was at this point I think I finally passed out.
I can feel they're moving me .   . the one that was holding
my shoulders puts my clothes back on. He moves neatly. I
offer no resistance. He dresses me. I hardly move . . he
was the only one that didn't take his clothes off .   . I mean
he didn't undo his flies .   . He's nervous and upset because
he didn't get a 'fuck' . . he's blubbering like a
disappointed child, but I can sense his haste . . . his fear.
He doesn't know what to do about the ripped sweater
he tucks the two strips into my trousers.

The van stops long enough for them to throw me out .
and then drives off.

I'm outside. I'm clutching at my jacket with my right hand
to cover my bare breasts.

It's nearly dark. Where am I? Plants .   . green .
grass . .
I'm in the park.

I feel ill. I mean I feel as if I'm going to pass out .   . it's not
just the physical pain . . . it's the degradation .   . the
humiliation . . . it's their spit on my face .   . the sperm
trickling out of me.

I lean my head against a tree . . . even my hair hurts . .
Yes, they were yanking my hair to keep my head still.
I wipe my face with my hand . . . covered with blood.
I turn up my jacket collar.
I walk in no particular direction . . . I just walk . . .

I find myself in front of the police station.
I lean against the front wall of the building, looking at it for
a long time.

I think about what I'd have to cope with if I went in
I can hear the questions.
I can see their faces .   . the smirks
I think about it.
I think about it some more.
And then I make my mind up
I'll go home.
I'll report it in the morning.

translated by GILLIAN HANNA

Alice in Wonderless Land

Fly! Fly! Alice .... But where are you flying to? Why are
you flying? You're still falling down . . . tumbling . . .
you're flying! Again! You're not a baby any more, Alice.
And you're still falling down holes. Huge deep holes that
open up in front of your feet in the meadows. You should
be ashamed of yourself. At your age! Still running after
bunny rabbits . . How old are you Alice for heavens'
sake? You're a woman now. You're not a little girl any
more. You can't go stumbling along like this any more – not
looking where you're putting your feet. When on earth are
you going to grow up Alice?

A-a-a-li-i-i-ce! Sto-o-o-p! When are you going to have
done with all this flying? This tumbling down?   . Look at
you with your skirt up round your ears . . . Cover yourself
up Alice. You're showing everything you've got! You could
at least change your knickers . . . put on clean ones . .
And what about your socks? They're absolutely filthy. You
ought to be ashamed of yourself .   what on earth will
people say? You little hussy! Stop!

Who's that shouting? All I can hear is a lot of shouting. I
can't stop. I just can't stop myself. Anyway I don't really
care. Actually I rather like falling . . . it's great! The wind is
stroking me, lifting my skirt up – I like it – it's pulling at
me. I like it! It's undressing me. I li-i-i-ke it!! Yes, yes I'm
sha-a-amele-e-ss . . . I like it! These hands are trying to
hold me back . . . who do they belong to? This one's my
father's hand. I recognise it . . . so strong . . . Let go of me
Daddy. My blouse is being pulled off . . . it's gone!
Another hand, no two hands . . . they're kind. It's my
mother. A smack . . . she smacked me . . . "A disgrace to

your family" she shouted at me . . . I'm falling .   . another
hand: it's my husband. Let me go! My skirt . . . my skirt's
being pulled off . . . it's gone! I'm flying. I'm flying again!
More hands: a policeman, a judge, a teacher, a priest! They've
pulled all my clothes off .   . I'm naked .   . I'm falling through
the air completely naked .   . the hole's getting narrower.
It's like being inside someone's intestines. It's like sliding on
a toboggan. Round and round .   . My head's spinning . . .
my stomach's turning round and round .   Oh God I think
I'm going to be sick .   . I'm throwing up . . . eueugh!, now
I've landed on a chair with such a bump! Crash! Who's this
sitting opposite me? A rabbit in a top hat drinking tea . .
I'm sick in his face   'Oh dear. I do beg your pardon.'

Think nothing of it. It's polite to take one's hat off in the
presence of a naked lady. Hip hip hurray! At long last – a
naked woman .   . a liberated lady! Please, please, my dear,.
vomit away to your heart's content. Do whatever you like
with that delicious little mouth of yours. What on earth are
you doing with your hands though? Covering yourself up?
Don't tell me you're ashamed .   Oh you're doing that to
turn me on. Oh yes yes .   . those slender fingers just letting
a little peep of breast show through .   . And the other
fingers down on the belly .   . oh I'm getting all excited .
it looks as if you're touching yourself .   . yes, yes, go on,
touch yourself . . . Oh just hold on a moment, here are my
guests: piglet and monkey. How nice to see you! Please
make yourselves at home. Allow me to introduce you to
Alice. She's an actress. She makes erotic films. Isn't she
gorgeous? Alice this monkey is a very well known avant-
garde film director. He's out of work just now: oh just look
at him wanking .   . yes he's scratching his head .   Well
that's his way of wanking. He's an intellectual. He's
suffering from ontological insecurity. Hang on, don't run
away. Hey Alice, stop!

Let go of me .   . piglet, take your hands off me

Oh do calm down, no one wants to hurt you. No violence.
We're opposed to all forms of violence. The director just

wants to film you. He wants to make a film about liberation
. . . it's the story of an extremely sensual young woman,
positively bursting with *joie-de-vivre*. She rejects all the
conventions of a repressive rule-bound society . . . It's a
delicious story of rebellion against petty bourgeois
patriarchal morality .   This woman discovers her own
body, her own identity .   . the pleasure of touching herself
   . of stroking herself . . . giving herself pleasure . . . go
on, touch yourself, stroke yourself .   . Be quiet piglet, this
is art . . . keep that big cock of yours out of this. Get
behind the camera and start filming. Now, as I was saying
   . this woman .   . is discovering herself .   . and they
marry her off to a real pompous twit . . . a male chauvinist
pig who slaps her around. And what does she do? She runs
away. Just like you ran away. But there are other men:
sneaky types who try to snare her with insidious tactics:
they pretend to be all sweetness and gentleness, they cajole
her. They praise and flatter her. They bewitch her. They
put you on a throne and adorn you with beautiful robes – all
the better to undress you! They tell you about liberation
and the dignity of woman and then wham! They screw you!

Run Alice! Run away! .   . You're stumbling . . . falling
into another hole . . . fly away and then bump! . . . Look
here you are with your sisters .   . other women struggling
for liberation, just like you. It's good, really good to be
together, talking, debating . . . but they're saying things
you can't always understand. They make you feel a bit
inadequate . . . ah, you see there's a boss here too. A
woman who tells you what to do and what to think . . .
she's after power too . . . But they're not all like that. One
of them is very fond of you . . . She loves you, yes she
really loves you . . . What are you doing Alice? You hadn't
expected that? No, no homosexuality isn't wicked. No it's
not a sin. Quite the opposite. It's beautiful . . . liberated
. . . Running off? Oh dear. You're positively stuffed full of
ridiculous prejudices . . . What a reactionary education you
must have had . . . Running away? Where are you going?
Alice, stop. Don't run. Be careful, there's another hole. A

huge gaping hole . . . you've fallen in, Alice! You're falling!
Fly, fly Ali-i-i-i-ce! It's lovely. It's lovely. The wind's twirling
you round and round. Your hair's flying! Look out. You're
getting near the ground .   . a huge meadow   . long grass
   . bump . . . oh such a gentle bump. You're still bouncing
   . rolling. What's this licking your face? A dog, oh what a
lovely doggie! He's a sheep dog. Hasn't he got lovely eyes?
You stroke him. He wants to play. He's jumping up at you. He's
rolling over to please you. He wants you to run with him.
Run Alice! Go on, run! Laugh! Shout! Oh what an adorable
dog. You fall over, and he lies down beside you   . isn't he
affectionate? Alice .   . this doggie simply adores you. He's
so sweet. He'd die for you. He'll look after you .   Did
you see the way he jumped up and growled at that man who
wanted to take you away? He's biting the man. The man's
running away! The dog's coming back to you. He's licking
your hands. Go on, why don't you make love with him . .
With the dog. The dog is the furthest shore . . . Love with a
beast . . with the beast lurking inside each of us .   we all
have a beast inside us .   Especially women. Go on, Alice.
Don't hesitate   . Behave yourself piglet . . . it's the dog
fucking, not you. You go and fuck the monkey.
Intellectuals suffering from ontological insecurity are all the
bloody same. Alice what are you doing with that stick?
Beating the dog? But he's man's best friend . . . you've hit
him on the head .   . you've killed the dog! The erotic
doggie . . . and the job we had to train him! No, hey what's
it got to do with us? Leave it out will you. Put that stick
down. No, aaargh! Look, I'm just a poor bunny rabbit in a
top hat. I'm an artist, dammit! Calm down, will you. Let's
have a cup of tea. Let's talk, let's discuss it! No, no don't
smash the camera . . . You're smashing it   . look if you
want to relieve your feelings, that's fine, have a go at the
monkey, but leave the camera alone. Alice stop it. Where
are you going? That's the enchanted forest over there.
Don't go in there, Alice. No, the Cheshire Cat lives in there
 . . . he laughs and fades away . . . And the Jabberwock's in
there . . . and the White Knight in Shining Armour
with his vorpal blade .   . wait, don't run!

I will run, you filthy beasts, so there! . . . Better the
Jabberwock than you lot – you screwed up bunch of rabbits,
monkeys and pigs! Oh what a beautiful forest! So many
trees . . . straight trees . . . crooked trees with branches like
arms! Oh my God! There's a tree taking me in its arms . . .
lifting me up . . . very gently . . . Ah, it has such soft leaves
– so moist . . . and such sweet smelling flowers . . . ah the
gentle rustling in the leafy branches . . . it sounds like a
love song . . . and the luscious fruit bursting out of their
skins . . . the sweet delicious juice dribbling out. I'm
drinking it . . . drinking it . . . That's enough now, thank
you. I get indigestion if I drink too much before meals. You
can put me down now . . . no, no thank you . . . What are
you doing? Oh how could you? The tree is panting . .
gasping . . . moaning . . . Oh no! . . . No! What do you
think you're doing to me? Get your filthy branches off me!
A tree with a penis? He-e-e-lp! Oh thank goodness,
someone's coming to rescue me. It's the Knight in Shining
Armour. And he's got his vorpal blade. Thwack! Wham!
Splat! A branch crashes down with every whack! Chop!
Chop! Chop off this filthy thing that's desperately trying to
shove itself inside me. Aaargh! A scream. The tree's bent
double . . all its branches down there lopped off . . it's
been castrated. Oops, it's dropped me down onto the
meadow. Here's a mushroom sprouting. Skipping round
me, puffed up and shiny! Give it a kick . . . Wham! Gotcha!
Ha ha! Off he goes hopping and howling like a mad dog!
What a world! Can it really be true that you've all got sex
on the brain . . . nothing but sex? Every last one of you –
and that includes trees and mushrooms! Where's the Knight
got to? Vanished. And his beautiful prancing steed has
vanished too . . . that's a pity. I'd like to have said thank
you to him at least. Blissful silence. Peace. At long last.
Golly, I'm hungry! Well there's fruit on those trees . . No,
better not risk that again . . . What on earth is this
contraption coming along the path? A fridge? A self-
propelled fridge on wheels! Oh stop! Do stop, fridge!
Thank you very much. I wonder if I could have a peep and
see what you've got inside you? May I open your door? Oh

you've got everything! Cheese, eggs, milk . . . there's even
some meat! O heavens, I'd love a steak . . but how am I
to cook it? Oh how wonderful, here comes a complete
kitchen with cookers . . . and saucepans . . . and frying
pans. There's even a dishwasher and a washing machine.
And a hoover . . No, stop. What are you up to? Help! I'm
surrounded. Stop pushing me. You're squashing me . .
OK. Yes, I'll use you all, but one at a time. No-o-o. You're
suffocating me. Oh where's the White Knight? Here he
comes! Thank goodness. Take that! And that! Snicker
snack! Splat! What a whack! He's smashing them to
smithereens! O thank you. They're all disappearing. All
these electric gadgets vanishing into thin air . . . no . . no
. . . don't smash the fridge. Wham! Too late! He's pulverised
it! Disaster. Not a single egg saved. Knight! . . . Hold on a
minute . . stop! Where are you going? Hahaha . . .
hahaha . . who's that laughing? Who is laughing like that?

A cat? Oh yes, of course, it's the famous Cheshire Cat,
that's who's laughing. He laughs and then he disappears.
He's vanishing bit by bit. First his tail, then his eyes, then
his paws, then his body, till all that's left is the grin. Then
the grin vanishes and all that's left is . . . what's this
thingummy? A cat's willy? Oh my God no. That's
impossible. This is becoming an obsession. Maybe *I'm*
obsessed. It's me . . it's all my fault! I must be dreadfully
sick. I'm obsessed with sex. And I imagine penises and
copulation and violence everywhere. Calm down will you.
Calm down. Concentrate. Be sensible. Come on now, close
your eyes, relax, take a deep breath. Let your thoughts go.
Concentrate on your feet. Count the toes . . one by one
 . up a bit . . now concentrate on the knees . . up a bit
more . . skip the pubes . . the stomach . . . concentrate
on the stomach . . . the breasts . . think about the breasts
 . . . not too much . . . throat . . . mouth . . ears . .
There we are. That's better. I feel much better. Relaxed.
Now drop the head. Lift the head. Drop down over the
toes. Eeegh! Who's touching my bum? The Knight! Thank
heavens! I thought it was a tree. Or a mushroom. Or a cat.

So. So? And what are your intentions, Knight?
Honourable? Well let's hope so. You'd like to take me in
your arms? All right – watch out! You're scratching my skin
with all your armour plating. Don't forget I've got nothing
on. On horseback! How lovely to ride on horseback! Clop,
clop clop. It's like being in a fairy story. And where are you
carrying me off to? To your castle? What do you mean you
haven't got a castle? . . Well what's that concrete thingie
over there that looks like a factory? It's a factory. Is it
yours? What sort of a Knight are you? An Industrial
Baron? Well what's your name then? Lord Zanussi?

I hope you're not going to try and make me work in there.
Look. I'm warning you, I haven't the slightest intention . .
I'll be being worked on. What do you mean, 'worked on'?
What's this? A conveyor belt? No   no . . . I'm sliding
along a conveyor belt. I'm on the assembly line   aaargh
 . rollers under my back   jerking along .   running
 . I'm slipping!

What are all these workers round the conveyor belt up to?
What are they doing to me? Get your hands off me! They're
opening me up, they're taking me to bits! Taking a load of
stuff out of me .   . and putting a whole load of different
stuff back in. 'Reconstruction! Conversion! Modernisation!'
Oh I recognise this bit they've taken out. 'Sense of common
decency'. They're putting something else in instead:
'Liberating uninhibitedness'! Oh that's nice! What are they
taking out now? 'Female eunuch's castration complex'
'otherwise known as anguish or penis envy'.   Oh yes, for
heaven's sake get rid of that. Thank you. Hey, what about
putting something else back instead? 'Maternal pride' But
I've already got that . . . do me a favour will you . .   What
about 'Uterine self-affirmation allied to ovarian self-
confidence'? Haven't got any? What do you mean sold out?
What sort of factory is this anyway? I bet it's one of the
Government's Enterprise Initiatives! Oh well, let's make do
with sexual self-determination for want of anything better.
Yes, yes away with all the antique hang-ups. Away with the
inferiority complex as well. That should have gone out with

the ark . . . and the Oedipus Complex as well . . . Not that
one? Why? Are you sure? But . . . OK . . . we won't have
an argument. Hang on a minute, don't close it up yet.
You're not going to leave me without a developed sense of
self-esteem and self-gratification? And what about
psychological self-sufficiency? Oh, I see. It's all here in
these three valves. Thank heavens for that. Right. OK . . .
They get implanted in my brain. Look, watch that drill will
you? God, what a headache. Finished? My that was quick!
What? Oh, of course, automation! Now what are you up
to? The packaging. What packaging? Look I'm not a *thing*.
Dear Lord, I'm a woman. I'm a conscious woman and I
have some dignity. You have to understand that I'm proud
to be a woman now! Conscious! No, not tights! Oh God,
no. I don't want to put them on. They're sexually
oppressive! Anyway they're unhygenic. They're itchy . . .
They irritate my skin . . . Oh all right, as long as you put in
a self sticking panty liner allowing me complete freedom
and confidence. Oh yes . . the anti-cellulite cream, the
light-control girdle, the famous cross your heart uplift bra
. . . odourless hair removing cream . . phpht! Twenty-four
hour deodorant . . slimming pills . . . contraceptive pills
. . all over body spray . . . anti-dandruff hair mousse . .
sparkling health salts to clean out the system . . . hormone
capsules to make your pee pure and transparent . . . paste
to give you a ring of confidence . . ointment to develop
the bust . . shoes like gloves . . with stiletto heels to tip
the arse forward . . and destroy your ovaries . . . false
eyelashes. Nail varnish. Scarlet lipstick. Rouge . . .
Eyeshadow . . . Violet for the eyelids. A plaster for your
corns .   Two dabs of perfume . . . Chanel . . . flannel . .
Rev-lon . . A-von . . rave on . . . come on!

There you are. Thank you Madame! That's all! You're
beautiful. You're free. You're young. Modern. Adorable.
Desirable. Antiseptic. Sterilised. Desexed . . . What a
fucking carve up!

translated by GILLIAN HANNA

The Whore in the Madhouse

A woman is sitting on a metal chair. She has earphones on and a microphone in front of her mouth, and a series of wires attached to her ankles and wrists. They run into a machine, valves and lights which flash on and off intermittently.

Yes, yes Doctor, I can hear you. I can hear you fine. Don't worry. I am relaxed. It's just that I feel a bit like a robot . . . it's all these wires. Actually to tell you the truth I feel like I'm sitting in an electric chair . it feels dreadful, really it does . . . Listen, Doctor, wouldn't it be better if you came over here and sat by me instead of being stuck inside that space capsule thing? Because I can't talk to someone about certain things if I can't see their face . while I'm talking. Like this – well I feel like I'm in a rocket being shot to the moon! I'll still tell you the truth wherever you're sitting. You can't? You've got to stay over there so you can keep an eye on the machine? OK, OK. If you can't, you can't . Well where do you want me to begin? From when we set fire to the industrialist's place? No? Prostitute? From when I became a prostitute? Listen Doctor, I don't like saying that word – prostitute – I'd rather say 'whore' to tell you the truth. I mean I think it's better to be straight, don't you?

All right, yes. OK. Yes. Yes I understand. My first sexual experience . the first . I can't remember . I can remember the second . well I can't remember the first because I was too small . . my mother told me about it while she was having a row with my father and that's how I found out that my father had tried to rape me . . but I

don't remember it . . . No, no trauma. I loved my father.
The second one . . . yes, that one . . . well I've already told
you all about that, haven't I? Yes with a boy in a field
behind our house. The grass was soaking wet and my
backside was really freezing. God he was green. He was
thirteen and I was twelve . . . It was the first time for both
of us. All we knew was that babies come out of the
stomach. No, nothing. I didn't feel a thing. Oh yes, now I
remember my belly button really hurt. Yes, my belly
button, because we thought that's where you made love . . .
and he kept pushing his thingie into it . . . I told you he was
green .   . gave me a swollen belly button. You've got no
idea . .   Yes of course I know what sexuality is . . . phhh
.   . oh come on, Doctor, I'm not as dumb as I look you
know . . . As a matter of fact, I'm rather well informed . .
I've read loads of books on sexuality .   . scientific books
too . . . That's how I found out that we women've got
erogenous zones .   . that's what they're called, isn't it,
Doctor? . . . Erogenous .   . we've got erogenous zones all
over our bodies .   . That was a real eye opener for me I
can tell you. I never dreamed that women had so many
sensitive erogenous spots: I came across one book that had
a diagram of a naked woman divided up into four parts . .
just like those posters you see hanging up in the butchers –
a cow chopped up into joints . . . like a map of the country
with all the counties and towns marked in . . . And every
area of this woman's body – in this book – was marked in a
different colour, graded according to its greater or lesser
sensitivity to male contact – I mean when they touch us . . .
I'll give you an example . . . this bit here, you see, the loin,
was coloured all red . . . that means it's the most erogenous
you can get. Then this bit here, behind the neck, that was
all mauve. You know, the bit they call 'best end' in the
butchers. Then this bit down the back, that would be the
fillet, was all little orange dots. Then lower down, the
backside, the rump . . . oh the rump, now that really was
something . . . *crème de la crème* as they say . . . Really
special . . . Well that's almost like 'sirloin'. Well it turns out
that if you know how to go about it, the 'sirloin' will give

you erotic shivers that'll blow the top of your head off! You see now Doctor, aren't I clever? I know everything there is to know about women's sexuality. Yes I know it all. But I'm a fool all the same. No, worse than a fool, I'm an idiot. You could say I've got a screw loose somewhere   . I'm not just saying that, Doctor, it's just that I always see the funny side of things .   And you know Doctor, there are times when I suddenly haven't the foggiest what's going on, and then I do things and afterwards I can't remember what I've done. Well I know because people tell about them later. What? What have they told me? But Doctor, we've been into all that already   . Oh that doesn't make any difference, I've got to tell you all over again . . . Oh I see, of course, so you can get it all down on the machine . . O my God, I just felt a shock, here   It's nothing? Hey, you're not trying to roast me alive, are you? Yes, yes   I'll go on

Well, people tell me that when I went out of my mind, I took all my clothes off and danced around naked. They screwed me naked. You don't say that? Well what do you say? They 'took' me? Yes, well, they 'took' me first and then they screwed me. Yes, OK I'm going on. Who? How many? Where? I don't know. I don't remember. All I know is that when I woke up here in the asylum they'd pumped me full of sedatives and I slept for two days on the trot and such bloody pain. It felt like I'd been given a good kicking .   . of course they'd kicked hell out of me   . . I was covered in bruises! Even on my face. How should I know, the police who picked me up say I'd fallen over. No they couldn't find any witnesses. When the police arrived to take me to the asylum emergency ward there was no one about   well if there was anyone, they'd only just arrived on the scene, or they were just passing by. But who gives a toss about me anyway? I'm a whore, right? A whore who throws a fit every once in a while. She goes berserk. Look I'm not giving you a sob story Doctor. Come on, everyone says the same thing anyway: what's a whore? A woman who's found a way of getting along very nicely thank you without doing any work! God, when I think about how hard

I worked! I was a maid and I got fucked! Then I worked in a factory and I got fucked there as well . . . Slag, you open your legs a damn sight too quick . . . anyone can see that you love every minute of it . . . bitch! No, no I *don't* love it . . . Yes I know it's too simple. It's too easy to lay all the blame on shitty blokes . . . it's all society's crappy fault . . . Even my own mother used to say to me: 'If you want to be a decent woman, there's no way out of it, you've got to kill yourself before you give in' . . . And I did kill myself . . . eight hours in the factory and then the overtime on top of that. Actually it was there I went out of my head. I had my first turn in the factory. I'd been there a week and I was having the most terrible hot flushes. My head was spinning . but the forewoman said I was making it all up, said I was kicking up a fuss so's I could get off sick. So in the end I just blew up. Smashed the windows with a trolley. Knocked over the drums of dye . . . and smeared myself all over with paint! And then they told me I began to dance naked up and down the corridors . . . Yes, the full stripper act . . . right into the management offices . . . and all the clerks howling with laughter and applauding like mad – those bastards! Are you kidding? Of course I hadn't a clue what was going on. Yes after I left Casualty they brought me here to the bin. And when the bin discharged me I'd lost my job . . . they'd discharged me too. The management. You can think what you like Doctor, but I'm telling you the God's honest truth, I didn't turn to whoring from choice. Look I've never met a single girl who'd rush up to you and say 'Oh it's a great life being a whore!!' No. What they all say is: 'I'm going to make myself a bit of money out of this stinking business and then I'm going to get out. Buy myself a little shop. A tobacconist's . . me and my bloke.' If only that was true, all the tobacconists' in the country would be run by whores.

One of the doctors here – she works on Ward Fifteen – you'd think she was just a schoolgirl to look at her – I've got friendly with her because I tell her everything – and she writes it all down. Well she explained to me that the reason

I go crazy is because I've got a guilt complex   because I
can't live with the idea of being a whore. I have a disorder.
What the fuck is a disorder? I don't know much about that
stuff, doctor, but all I'm telling you, and you can call me
mad if you want to, is that I even enjoyed being in that
factory. It was a knackering job but I liked being with all
the other women. The noise was unbearable, the heat made
you giddy, the solvents gave you a terrible headache and
the supervisor was a bitch   so I ask myself, what on
earth could you possibly enjoy about all that? I enjoyed it
because it gave me self-respect, that's what. What makes
this job so rotten is that it makes you feel like nothing but a
thing – a thing with a hole and legs, an arse, tits, a mouth
and that's all .   . nothing else. And if someone's up to their
ears in shit, what do they do? They keep swimming and
take no notice of the stink. And you try to keep your head
above water and find someone who'll keep you afloat
and it's one way of getting your revenge .   'Want to
screw, shitface? Who the hell do you think you are anyway,
just because you've got a couple of quid in your pocket? All
right then, pay up! Screw and pay up! I'm not here. You
can hump away as much as you like, but I'm not here. I'm
pretending to be here   but I've gone off somewhere
else. You're fucking a corpse, you bastard.'

In fact those are the times I really do go somewhere else,
that's when I do go right out of my head. That's when I
make an exhibition of myself and I start dancing around
stark naked .   . and finally you and your friends get stuck
in and slap me around .   you jump on me, five or six at a
time, you really let me have it .   . bastards .   . and all that
rotten hate you have for us – for women – it really comes
pouring out of you .   Now you feel like *real* men .
stinking bastards.

But the stinking bastard who did me a favour the last time,
I didn't forget him: a real big-shot. Company car, huge suite
of offices, dozens of secretaries, friends in high places .
all pigs just like him. But I pretended I wasn't there .
and then by chance I found myself in the wine bar under his

office one day when they were leaving work, and he's
always in there on the dot – like clockwork. So I did my
dumb bimbo act . . . just asking for it, bit of a giggle . . .
ready to go. A dab of perfume and fresh as a daisy. There
were a lot of other blokes from his crowd all offering to go
off with me so he joined in the competition and I let him
win: 'The gentleman has won a fuck! Congratulations sir!'
He's bursting with pride, sweeps me out of the bar winking
at all the poor losers. We go upstairs to his office with the
adjoining bedroom and he falls on me as if we're still
downstairs with all his slobbering mates watching him,
cheering him on: 'Go on, my son! Go for it! Great stuff . .
What a stud!' You'd have thought he had peacock feathers
sticking out of his arse. Then he suddenly keels over like a
dead ox. I get dressed and nick everything I can lay my
hands on: cheque book, car keys, office keys, keys to the
lift, to his house, to the garage, to the speedboat, to the
safe . . . passport, driving licence . . . all his cards: Rotary
Club, Shooting Club, American Express, Tory Party card
. . . the lot. I even took the Queen's Award for Industry
that he had framed over the desk between the portraits of
Maggie Thatcher and Princess Di.

Then I went on my merry way and came here to the asylum.
I told them that I felt one of my attacks coming on and they
admitted me . . . O I forgot to tell you I put a little note on
his desk before I left his office: 'If you want to find me I'm
in the emergency ward up at the mental hospital.' The
stinking bastard phoned up and got the admissions desk,
but the nurse on duty knew all about what had happened:
'Oh yes, you must be the gentleman who took advantage of
a sick woman?' A lawyer turned up at the asylum but they
threw the lawyer out. The bloke wanted to talk to me
alone, but I said if he wanted to talk to me he could come
into the ward and do it in front of all the other patients.
And when he got in, what a right little maggot he looked!
We put him on trial.

He had to confess everything that he and his bastard friends
had got up to with me ten days before. And he was shaking

like a leaf . . . and stammering .   . and blubbering . .
'And now we're going to tell the papers, we've got the
whole lot recorded on tape.' He had a fit. The fat pig! He
looked like he should be hung up in Smithfield market! And
then we gave him back all his stuff and sent a transcript of
the tape to the papers.

He must've been desperate. Went into overdrive. Christ
knows what he did for who or to whom, but the upshot was
that no one published a word of this sordid little story.

Five days later I was going out of the gate on my way home
and I noticed this car following me .   . I started to run, but
at the corner of the street two blokes jumped out of another
car and started to beat hell out of me, and they'd have
killed me, I'm not kidding, if two of the nurses hadn't
noticed what was going on from the porters' lodge and
come rushing out to help me. They took me up to Casualty
more dead than alive.

Later all my chums from the asylum carried me back to the
ward. They were all crying .   . not out of pity .   . out of
fury. 'Jesus Christ   ' they were sobbing 'They despise us
 . . they screw us .   . they beat us and we're supposed to
take it with a smile on our faces. Well we'll get those
bastards this time!'

'It's pointless' the young doctor said. 'Trying to get revenge
is pointless . . . You can only achieve anything through
organised political struggle, my friends, not individual acts
of vengeance'.

'Who said anything about vengeance?' We all said. 'What
we have in mind is just that: a political action.' The next
evening a fire broke out in the middle of town. The posh
building where that bastard has his office went up in flames.
'Arson' they said on the TV. 'Political action' said one of
the inmates. 'Political action' replied all the others. The
young doctor was silent for quite a while . . . and then she
said: 'Yes, a political action.'

translated by **GILLIAN HANNA**

Coming Home

*A woman mimes getting off a bus . . . screech . . . brakes
. . . the bell rings. She looks round . . she's been jostled.
She has trouble getting her bearings.*

Bleedin' fog . . where's the name . . . ah here it is . .
'Gaitskell House . . Clement Atlee Estate . .' So it must
be over here . . careful now . . it'd be easy to get the
wrong block in this fog . . . Bleedin' blocks, they all look
the bleedin' same! You'd think they'd have painted them
different colours – stripes, dots, squares . . parallelograms
. . . little flowers . . . but no, rows and rows of bleedin'
little boxes . . and every one the same shit-green colour!

She turns to the audience.

This is it – the exact spot – the exact precise moment when
the balloon went up and my life went hurtling off the rails
into total disaster. I was already a bit upset anyway . . .
God, I don't know whether I'm coming or going . . the
entire day spent in bed with a man . . . yes, me! A married
woman with two kids. In a hotel bedroom. And it's not
even as if I was that crazy about him . . . Well, he wasn't
even my lover or anything! Actually, I hardly even knew
him . . . well I mean I did know him before . . . but I only
got to know him properly today . . . a bit too properly if
you ask me.

It's all my husband's fault . . . it's all his fault I'm up shit-
creek without a paddle . . .

Well anyway, this Horace . . . yes, I'm telling you, that's
the bloke I've been tangled up in bed with for hours . . . I'd

barely even set eyes on him before. He's just a bloke who works in the same office as me. Yes, not bad looking . . Actually he's rather handsome .   . But you see, to tell you the truth, 'handsome' isn't the be all and end all .   . there's a whole load of other things got to come into it as well . For starters, there's got to be that little something .   . I don't know, the way he walks .   . something in the tone of the voice . . . the way he looks at me – you know, some little thing that presses all the right buttons and turns the lights on and bingo! .   . But Horace, well . . nothing! Horace had all the magnetism of a snail having a kip.

And anyway Horace doesn't smell right. Doesn't that ever happen to you? If a man – or even a woman come to that – just doesn't have the right smell . . . you know, the proper 'bouquet'   . . then it's a dead duck from the start. There's no stopping me when it comes to smells . . . I sniff everything and everyone . . . Someone only has to pass by – that's it, I'm off: sniff sniff .   . instant X-ray by nose.

What I'm saying is this Horace was a total non-starter even in the smell department . . . he didn't smell of anything .   . he was like an icicle!

And the only bit of him that I did know anything about was the bit that used to stick out of the cashier's window . Yes, Horace is the chief cashier. A bust. It never occurred to me that he might have legs and feet underneath. He was always 'Half Horace'.

Yes of course I'd noticed he used to give me the once over . actually he used to track me down like a bloodhound . he'd lift up his paw .   . slowly, ever so slowly, his neck'd go rigid .   we'd say good morning . . . and a huge arm would shoot out of his window, grab my hand and crush it like a nutcracker .   . Why is it that all men are obsessed with proving their virility by crushing your metatarsals . . . and then for hours afterwards you've got to type one-handed!!

Here we are .   . this is the first block .   . or maybe it's the second . . . here's the sign . . . if you could ever read it of course . . . in all this fog . . . Area O. Row 2. Well that 2 could be a 9 . . . and the O could be a Q . . . and if this is Q9 I'm buggered. It means I'm on exactly the wrong side . . three miles from home.

Maybe the Old Bill will come by . . . On second thoughts, the only reason the Old Bill would come by here is if he's lost too.

I could stop someone . . . oh yeah, great idea! It'd be just my luck to run into a sex maniac out taking advantage of the fog . . . he'd leap on me, rape me in a patch of grass in among all the dog shit . . . and then he'd leave me stark naked in the gutter . . . after he'd swiped my handbag of course. And that would really put the tin lid on this lousy day I've had . . the grand finale to this shitty day . . . Oh my God, it's enough to drive you screaming round the bend!

It got off to a really good start this morning with a flaming bust-up with my husband . . . about the way we'd made love the night before . . . well, when I say 'we' made, that's just a figure of speech . . . he does all the making round here.

I got as far as twenty-one . . . I always count when he starts in on the bed business . . . and that was it, he was over and done . Yes, in twenty-one seconds . .

What I'm saying is he treats me as if I'm one of the kids' video games . . . I'm the big yellow fish you have to chase into the blue maze . . hop, hop hop . . . and gobble it down quick . . gnum gnum . . . gotcha! . . . yum, yum!

And then I had to go to the bathroom for a wash . . . slap slop slop . . . And I go back into the bedroom . . . and look at him . . . he's fast asleep already . . . flat out with his arse sticking up in the air . . . So I rip off the blankets . . . grab one of his Nike Roadrunners: WHAM! A bloody great whack on his backside. He screams like a raging bull . . . and the neighbours are banging on the walls and the ceilings

. police sirens. All right everybody shut up! That's enough! The party's over for tonight. But at 6.38 this morning when the bleep bleep of the electronic alarm clock woke him up . . . there was I . . glaring at him . . . and I gave him the lot . . the sum total of everything I'd totted up on my pocket rage calculator: 'I'm not going to let you lay a finger on me ever again! I've had it up to here with you! I'm not going to be used as your slop bucket any more. I'm wiping the word "humiliation" out of my brain. I'm going to get my own back! I'm going to go on the game in front of that shop where you prat about pretending to earn a living, and I'm going to kick up a stink the like of which you've never seen! I'm going to stand in front of the window beside all that other crap you sell with a placard saying "For sale: wife of Mr Rogers, retail sales, washed and deodorised, full working order. Amazing reductions for Labour Party members, student nurses and UB40 holders . Closed Saturday and Sunday".'

All this time I was getting dressed. I was so furious I didn't even notice that I'd put on a blue and silver lamé and lace number. And I was making myself up as if I was going to a fancy dress ball instead of the office. And in between insults I was hurling everything I could find that was mine into a holdall.

I'd packed my bags a few times before, but as soon as I'd got into the lift – or down to the ground floor at the most – I'd always turned round and gone back. But not this time! The count-down was unstoppable! I felt like a guided missile . . on the launch pad . . . Ready to be fired . . All done up in lamé and lace. I already had smoke billowing out from under my skirt!

'All systems go for take-off into the Universe.'
'Don't drag the kids into this . . Still less your mother! It's too late now! Engines are go . . Countdown!   '

Husband's voice: 'All right then, go, why don't you.'

Wife's voice – mine: 'Minus thirteen and counting . twelve . .'

'And don't come back!'

'Eleven . . . ten . . . Of course I won't come back . . . do you think I'm going to hang about here and give you a chance to run me over on a zebra crossing? Nine . . EIGHT!!'

'I can find as many men as I want . . . men who'll respect me . . . love me . . . won't just use me when they feel like it . . Seven . . . six! And don't you stand there smirking you self-satisfied bastard. I can find them. Actually I've found some already . . . yes, that's right I've been unfaithful to you! SIX . . . FIVE! . . . well that wiped the smile off your face, didn't it? Unfai-ai-aithfu-u-u-l! Four . . . THREE!! Only they do it with a bit more style than you . . . hop hop hop! You precious twenty-one second fiasco! . . . Two . . one! Lift-off!! We have lift-off!! Vroooom! Vrooom! One thousand metres and still rising!'

She sings at the top of her voice.

'O husband mine,
O do not weep,
If I should lea-eave you-hoo-oo .   Vroom! Vroom!
I'm in orbit! Ten thousand metres .   . Hu-u-usband .   . I
can hardly see you.

'You look a bit upset, dear . . . a bit wobbly . . . I think you'll just have to put up with it . what do you think about that?

'God, what a disaster you lot have turned out to be these last few years. All those little floozies of yours . . . well it's true . . these days girls drop their knickers in a flash . . . but they put them back on just as fast and trolly out of the door leaving you with a cold bum on the floor. They're so available:

'Fancy a kiss?'
'Sure, let's kiss!'
'Fancy a fuck?'
'Sure, let's fuck!'

'And you still haven't got it into your thick heads that they're the ones who are fucking you .   . you're screwed and double screwed!

'And to think that all you're after is a bit of tender loving care, poor babies!

'Bloody women! Bloody bitches!'
Whee! You look so far away!
Oh God, my head's going round .   .   '

Change of tone.

Oh hell, it really is going round, with all the muck I've been knocking back all day . .
All right, that's enough loafing about doing sod all .   I've got to make my mind up . . . I've got to go home.
And how am I supposed to face them after that scene with the missiles this morning?

Maybe it'd be better if I waited here in the street .   . it . must be just about time for him to get home too . . . I don't want to get into a fight in front of his mother and the kids .

Oh hell, now I come to think of it, I walked out this morning without even saying goodbye to them

'Your mother can bring up the kids .   . She'll be right in her element now   . not having me under her feet any more .   '

I must have really gone into orbit this morning .

I trollied out of the house .   . dragging that bloody bag behind me . . . I was still in a right state when I got to the office . . . actually I never got as far as the office . . . I stopped at the wine bar on the corner . . . disaster these new opening hours, you know . . . leading young office workers astray . . . I felt a hand on my shoulder. It was him, Horace. The Hand Mangler. Only this time he was making do with crushing my shoulder blade .   .

I looked at him .   . Crikey!! He was a whole person .   . I

mean he had legs as well. He invited me to join him at a
table. He clocked that I was gobsmacked. I gave him a
quick sniff on the side. Well, he smelt better than usual.
He'd got hold of one of my hands, and he was managing to
stroke it without breaking any bones. He was gazing at me,
but with a different expression: he didn't look like a boiled
sheep's head . . Actually he looked quite nice . . . yes .
rather tasty . . . Maybe it was me .   . maybe I just
happened to be in the right mood .   . of course the two dry
martinis I'd poured down my throat must've helped.

'It's getting late. We ought to go up to the office,' he says to
me .   wolfing down two huge bread rolls as if they were
Junior aspirin.

'The office? No chance. Not today. I feel too ill. I've got to
go for a walk . I've got to get some air.'

'I'll go with you.'

'Thanks.' I gulped down the Campari he'd ordered in one
go – no lemonade – I might as well have swallowed a glass
of petrol . . We're outside . . . we're walking. God,
there's a blast of cold air whistling right up my skirt! What
the hell did I think I was doing putting on this lace and lamé
number? My backside's freezing. My feet are killing me and
I've got a thick head

We're in Kings Cross, and I remember that I've got trousers
and a jumper in the bag. There's a hotel right in front of us.

''Ere listen shall we go in?' He gapes at me. He's so pale I
think he's going to pass out. 'I'm cold .   . and I've got to
put on something a bit warmer.' I go in. He follows me. I
show them my Access card. He does the same. His hands
are shaking. Not me. I'm mega-cool. I'm off my head! I'm
completely off my head! 'I'll make you pay! I'll make you
pay for those twenty-one seconds! Kids!! Your mother's a
slag!'

Indescribable smell in the corridors: wellington boots, stale
smoke, tom cats. Disgusting room: the stink of two
thousand bonkings suspended in mothballs.

Before I can make my mind up to take my clothes off I smoke three cigarettes. Then I have second thoughts and I jump under the sheets fully dressed . . minus the shoes.

'What the hell am I doing up here?' There are two little bedside cupboards . . . I keep expecting the doors to burst open and my two kids' heads to pop out shouting: 'Mum! Mum! Don't do it! Don't do it!!'
Suddenly I sneeze . . my feet are frozen . . I'm beginning to get a sore throat too.

'O Christ, I'm going to get ill here . . I'm going to die in this room . . with this hand-mangler I hardly know!'

I turn my head to look at him: he's as naked as the day he was born!!

'You've taken all your clothes off!' What's he up to now?

With one bound he hurls himself on the bed . . to grab me! I just manage to dodge out of the way . . Wham! Horace smashes straight into the picture of the Queen hanging over the bed! What an arsehole! He's so dazed he starts saluting it . . . Then he picks himself up and starts trying to grab hold of me again.

'Stop!' I shriek 'Horace, one moment please! For six years all I've seen of you is your upper half. For two years you've been shaking my hand. For two hours I've been chatting to you . . . and after only five minutes together in a bedroom you leap on me stark naked? What are you? Some kind of sex maniac?'

Well that seemed to upset him. All hell breaks loose!! Horace bursts into tears and starts howling like a baby! 'What sort of kick do you get out of making an idiot out of me? You're destroying me . . . Christ, I've got enough woman trouble on my plate without you starting in on me . . . I'm practically impotent . . now you want to chop my balls off altogether!'

So then, in between heart-rending sobs, he pours out the story of his life . . . all his frustrations and neuroses going

back (naturally) to his childhood . . . At twenty-two he still
hadn't made his mind up whether he was A.C. or D.C. . .
so he didn't go out with anyone . . . he just J. Arthured like
a good'un   . even behind his cashier's window   .

At twenty-three he took up boxing in search of his
masculinity   . . and immediately fell hopelessly, madly in
love with his trainer Francis, an ex-welter-weight champion
. . . a barbarian who couldn't see the light of love in
Horace's eyes . . . he used to rough him up . . . and Horace
was too besotted to look out for himself . . . He had to give
it up after a few months because of the multiple fractures
and terrible swellings all over his face

At twenty-five he got married and separated in the space of
a month .   . to a good clean-living girl .   . she was a dental
mechanic

So now, having reached the age of thirty-five, he divided his
attentions and passions between Ali-Budhba, an Ethiopian
who's the barman in the pub beside Waterloo Station and
Tracy Rogers .   . from Peckham .   . that's me!!

Yes, I am Tracy Rogers in person! And I have just found
out that a barely breathing trunk of a man has been lusting
after me in silent desperation for years . . . I have been
his dream woman .   . the unattainable object of his
desire

Now I'm listening to him, and I'm smoking, I'm stupefied
. . . There was me thinking he was a dreary old fart .   .
This Horace .   . a man with no passion, no past .   . and
look what a tormented soul he turned out to be!

Well this really was a turn on!
He was holding both my hands very gently.

'You're the only woman I don't feel like running away from
   . I feel strong when I'm with you .   . I feel almost like a
man   '

'Wait and see, you'll find out that I'm Francis the welter-
weight boxing champion, Ali-Budhba the Ethiopian .

and the qualified dental mechanic as well .   . all rolled into one . . .'

I'm joking of course . . . but he just smiles at me .   . he doesn't even take offence.

I make the decision. I take my clothes off.

His face is still streaked with tears. I feel a bit awkward. If I haven't got the wrong end of the stick, I'm the first real woman he's ever had.

I can feel myself dripping honey from head to toe. I'm taking on a big responsibility here. What happens if I make a mess of it too?

We fall into each other's arms.

'It's OK!   . It's OK!   '

It's like being in a film . . . a film with dozens of frames missing .   . and then suddenly there are thousands too many . . . and they're from a different film altogether . . . Everything's rushing by . . . and then suddenly everything's in slow motion . . . I'm lying in cotton wool .   . I'm floating in the sheets. Our words slow down . . . our movements slow down . . . I'm breathing bubbles like I'm swimming in Babycham .   . My heart stops for minutes at a time.

Every now and then I try and get my breath back . . . but he catches me up again and carries me off in a whirl .   . up onto the mountain tops . . . It's so beautiful! Finding out about yourself is so beautiful! After twenty years of doubt he's starting his life again . . . he sighs . . . he trembles . . . he mutters strange phrases . . . O Christ . . . don't say I'm going to end up falling in love with Horace!

I stop him for a second:

'I'm warning you now, if you get carried away and call me Francis or Ali-Badhbu in a moment of passion, I'll open the window and throw you out!'

Well that was a stupid thing to say . . . it was a good job he was so neurotic already!

By the time we left the hotel it was dark. I'd put on the trousers and sweater I'm wearing now. I feel as if I'd had ten Turkish baths, two saunas and eight Swedish massages . . . I must have lost half a stone .   We go into a pub near the station.

'Two cherry brandies.'
'Want a bite to eat?'
'No thanks, I'm not hungry.'

He wolfs down three rolls, two sandwiches, four slices of cake and a bag of dry roasted

I'm going home. I get on the tube. When did I decide to do that? I'm pissed .   I force myself to keep my eyes open.

I have to get off at the Elephant. It's foggy   .

I come out and the bus is there already . . . It's about to go . And now here I am stuck in all this fog .

And my husband who's decided not to come home . .

Maybe he's gone in already .   . before I got back . . . I can't hang about like this any more .   . I'll go up. Staircase R. There's the lift. Am I really in the right place? I can't even get my bearings from the smell .   . everything always smells the same here: stink of dustbins, cat pee and disinfectant from the bogs. Once I made a mistake and ended up two blocks further over. I was still on the sixth floor. The door was open and I went in. Fortunately it was one of the flats with different fittings: white formica. You see we didn't get any choice about the colour of the fittings in these flats – like we didn't get any choice about the blackmail they get out of us for the rent – they only come in two sorts: white formica or red formica. I've got red formica.

Thank God the lift's already on the ground floor. The sixth floor button is the worn out one.

What a load of rubbish! Who the hell writes all this stuff . Oh, here's a new one:

'How many men does it take to tile a bathroom?' 'One . if you slice him thin . .'

Here we are. My glorious great landing . . . and here's the lovely big damp stain . . . and all the lovely flaking plaster that drops off the wall if you so much as glance at it

Kick the bloody wall! . . Christ, a bloody landslide!

Never mind, they'll blame the kids.

Take a deep breath . . preparatory to re-establishing my presence in the daily routine of my domestic shit-heap.

Put the right key in the lock of the right door. Bleedin' lock, it's forever sticking .

Ah, there we are . . . In we go . . . Pitch black as usual in the hall . . Aaargh!! What's that? The coatstand! So they've thrown it out already have they? That's nice! So you really thought I wasn't coming back, huh? Oh well, away with the good life . . let's start chucking all the furniture out!

Where are you then?! No answer? No one at home?

Oh there she is: Saint Mother-in-Law herself, knitting away under her twenty watt bulb – well she doesn't want to waste the electricity, does she?

She barely turns round.
'Is that you? Back already?'

This is obviously meant to get me riled . . . what she's saying is: 'Aha, bold as brass this morning, and now look at her, creeping back with her tail between her legs.'

'Ha, I'm not falling for that one . . . I'm not going to even deign to answer . . Lady Fair-Isle!'

Bleedin' heck, look what they've done to my kitchen . . . these plates are filthy . . these saucepans are disgusting . . . thick with grease . . . typical, you don't miss a chance do you . . taking advantage of a crisis . . . a poor woman finds herself wandering the streets in the bitter cold,

starving hungry, dressed in blue lamé and freezing her arse
off . . . she gets pissed on aperitifs . . . goes into a hotel
. hang on a minute, Trace! Walls have ears! .

OK! You lot! Come and wash up this festering heap of dirty
dishes! Now I see what's the matter . . they've got the
telly on. Ki-i-i-ids! Turn the sound down! How do you
expect me to tell whether you're home or not with that row
going on?! I said turn it down!

Now what's that? It's him! The old man coming in . . he
doesn't have to batter the door down!

Shh! I'd better keep my trap shut   better not to pass any
remarks .   . I think I'll stay in here out of harm's way
I'll keep a rolling pin handy   just in case

What are they up to now?

She listens.

Listen to the two of them, mother and her precious little
boy, nattering away. thick as thieves .   . that Welsh
mumbo-jumbo of theirs .   . they do it deliberately so you
can't understand a word they say   they're having a good
moan about me – as usual – It's enough to turn you into a
racist

God, someone's just got slapped. Which one was it? The
youngest – as usual! Well of course, of course it would be
    . because he's the one that takes after me! Well
do-o-one! That's it, go on . . . give it to the one that's least
able to stand up for himself!

Oh God, I'm shaking like a leaf .   . I can't breathe . . . I'm
one of those people who just can't take a whole day of
making love on an empty stomach in a sleazy hotel –
especially when I'm up to my eyebrows in Campari. What'll
I do? Drop dead right here?   No, better die in bed

Jesus, my head's buzzing .   . I'm ill .   . I can't undress
myself .   . I'll have to get under the covers the way I am
  . that makes it twice today I've got into bed fully dressed
  . Dear God, I must be in a bad way   I don't even

recognise the smell of my own bed . . . the pillow . . the
sheets . . . just a bleedin' minute! I can smell a woman . . .
and it's not me! Didn't waste any time, did he that bastard!
He's got another woman in already . . . What am I talking
about? In the afternoon? With Lady Fair-Isle in the sitting
room? Well I wouldn't put anything past that one. She'd
probably give Cynthia Payne a good run for her money .
she's already started hurling the furniture out . . Ooh my
head! I've got fireworks exploding in my brain . . the
room's going round . . . I'm going to throw up . . . What's
happened? They've all gone quiet out there! . Someone's
opened the bedroom door . . . they're peering at me . .
He's coming in! Who's that man? Don't be a berk, who do
you think it is? It's your husband.

What's going on now? Everything's gone wobbly . . . like in
a hall of mirrors . . The room's stretching out like a
corridor . my husband's all woozy . . . he's gone a funny
shape . . . what's he doing? Ah . . he's trying to give me
something to drink . . God I hope it's not another
Campari . . . no it's soup . . . I think . .

He said something under his breath . . . Can't understand a
word . . Oh well, let's get on with the soup . .

'What're you doing? No, whatever you do, don't turn the
light on . . . my head's exploding .   Yes, yes, let's stay in
the dark.'

He's here . . . he's sat down on the bed . . he's still for a
bit . . we sit here in silence.

'What the hell's that? Is that you touching my head?'

'Ah, you're stroking me . . . that's nice . . yes, yes, run
your fingers through my hair .   . that's so nice . . but
gently . . do it gently.'

'Is that you taking off my trousers? Sorry, I haven't a clue
what's going on . . . A second ago you were sitting up here
by my head. and now all of a sudden you're down at my
feet.'

'Yes, take my tights off . . . gently . . . oh that's so nice!'

God I feel as if I'd spent the day being whizzed up in a
blender. 'Yes, my jumper as well . . . oh I feel good . . .'
God I'm peeing myself! Oh no, I spilt the soup . . . all over
me .

'I'm sorry, I'm pissed'   . who said 'Me too!'
'You did?'
'It sounds like you're talking through a megaphone.
Go on, then, talk. Keep talking . . . I like that booming
sound . . . Have you been drinking too? Night Nurse and
brandy? You must be nuts! That stuff's lethal! Yes, yes . . .
I feel the same . . . first I get bigger and bigger, and then I
get smaller and smaller . . . my foot's over there . . . I've
got one hand on the ceiling . . . you're not angry with me
any more? After this morning?'

'Oh thank God! .   . No, me neither .   . Don't be silly .
All that crap I was coming out with.'

Peace! Sweet peace! Oh I'm so happy!
Ooh, I love my old man's smell tonight!   . sniff .   . sniff
   . ooh I love it!

What a day! What a night! All day with Horace . . . all
night with my husband! Non-stop lovemaking without a
breather!

That's it .   . from tomorrow on, I'm going to start drinking
like a fish . . . that'll really give Lady Fair-Isle something to
whinge about!

'What a way to carry on! It's not nice! A lady never drinks!
Disgraceful!'
Fabulous! How long is it since we made love like that!
It's probably my fault he sometimes only manages to keep it
up to twenty-one seconds.

It's up to me to light his fuse – that must be why he hasn't
been going off at all! Oh Jesus, I'm in a twelve programme
washing machine . . . I'm talking rubbish . . . I'm bursting
into bloom like a gorse bush . . . I'm sprouting blossoms

that'll drive hornets insane! And he's saying:

'It's great! It's wonderful you came back this evening. I wasn't expecting you till tomorrow at the earliest .   .'

'Liar! You threw all the furniture out! You and that mother of yours!'

'My mother can go to hell .   I love you! I love you!'

'I was unfaithful to you today .   . with a trunk of a man . . .'

'With who? Who cares .   I had it coming to me . . . hold me tight .   I want you .   I want you madly   '

'All right, but look out . . . if I see you thinking about Ali   . or the dental mechanic   '

'What the hell are you talking about?'
'Nothing . . . nothing . . I was kidding . . . I'm pissed   '
God, what a night! Sodom and Gomorrah had nothing on us!
'Don't make so much noise! You'll wake the kids up .
and your mother!'

'No, no never mind .   talk to me .   . scream .   ' I can't imagine anything more wonderful than waking her up .
her eyes out on stalks and her nails chewed down to the quick hearing her son making mad passionate love to me!

O God, he's starting all over again, the big bear! I've had it this time! I'm going . . . this time I'm really going to die
 . I'm going .   . ooh, what a way to go!

Pause.

Hmm! What? Where am I? Berk. I'm in bed. My bed. It's coming back to me .   . slowly .   . now let's take this slowly
 . it's slowly coming back to me .

What's that clattering?
Ah, knives and forks. What time is it? Maybe it's

dinnertime already . . . maybe they're all in there having lunch.

Bloody hell, I went out like a light!

Oh God, the office! Don't be daft, it's Saturday.

All right then, let's get this day on the road. I'm in a right state! Head like a lead balloon .   . muscles .   . bones . I'm wrecked all over.

'Shut up, you lot, your Mum's asleep!'

That's my husband's voice.

Bless him!
Well I'd better get up then. Dressing-gown? Where the hell's my dressing-gown? Oh never mind, I'll put on my trousers .   . sweater   . shoes?

Here   . Oh Lord, I've still got the staggers .

Open the door . . .
Jesus H. Christ! Who are all these people? All these strangers sitting round my dinner table?

A man who isn't my husband.
An old woman who isn't my mother-in-law.
Two children who aren't my children .   . and the cat in the armchair isn't mine either!

Oh God, they're all looking at me .   . gobsmacked! Like goldfish!!

Suddenly everyone looks towards the hall. The key is turning in the lock. The door's opening . . . A woman comes in. She's wearing an overcoat .   . she's carrying a suitcase.

'Mum! Mum!' the kids rush to meet her
Everyone's turning round to stare at me .   . I feel like a vegetarian at a sausage tasting .

I go to the coatstand .   . take down my coat .   . pick up the holdall .

'Sorry . . . there seems to have been a bit of a
misunderstanding . . . oh well, these things happen, don't
they?!'

translated by GILLIAN HANNA

Tales of the Resistance

Nada Pasini (1970)
The Eel-Woman (1970)
Mamma Togni (1971)
Fascism 1922 (1973)
An Arab Woman Speaks (1972)
The Bawd – The Christian Democrat Party in Chile (1973)

The first three monologues are drawn from the Italian Resistance.

Nada Pasini is taken from a first-hand account by Nada Pasini herself. *The Eel-Woman* comes from a tape-recording by a woman who took part in the formation of a Communist partisan group in the Po Delta. Both these are taken from the full-length drama-documentary *I'd Rather Die Tonight if I Had to Think it Had All Been in Vain* . . *Mamma Togni* is the story recorded by a legendary woman partisan from the Upper Po Valley near Pavia. The last of this group of three pieces is drawn from a collection of eye-witness accounts of resistance to Fascism around Novara in 1922–23.

The monologue by an Arab woman was taped and brought to Franca Rame by a comrade from Beirut. On a visit to the Lebanon Franca Rame had found it impossible to overcome the Arab women's reluctance to speak of their experiences; their lack of freedom as women was too deeply imprinted to allow them to accede to her request.

The Bawd was first performed in Sassari in Sardinia in 1973 a few weeks after the Fascist coup in Chile. Next evening Dario Fo was arrested, handcuffed and taken off to prison; an event that gives an idea of the political climate in Italy in those years. The piece was performed hundreds of times in public places all over Italy.

STUART HOOD

Nada Pasini

*'And afterwards? After we've chased out the Fascists . .
What will we do then? Are we going to manage to make this
revolution?' How many times do we find that question
repeated in the accounts that the partisans have left us. That
anxiety; that sense of desperation, almost.* Afterwards .
what are we going to do afterwards?

*It's this same question that we find in the following account
by Nada Pasini, a courier for the Seventh GAP of Bologna.
Here is her story.*

* * *

At Porta Lame on 7 November 1944, there was a big battle,
and thousands of Germans and Fascists were attacked by
the partisan forces of Bologna, en masse. The Nazi-Fascists
took a heavy beating. On the partisan side too there were
people killed, and a number of wounded . Seventeen of
them, the most seriously wounded, were taken off to a well-
concealed infirmary over towards Via Duca d'Aosta. But
the Fascist police, using spies and informers, managed to
discover the hideaway, and they staged a surprise raid on it.
Some of the wounded were killed immediately by the SS.
They were tied to the bars of the windows and beaten to
death. The others, attendants and nurses included, were
brutally tortured.

Then it came to my turn . Two militiamen took me up
into a big room where there were some Fascists, dressed in
civilian clothes. There was one man, with glasses, wearing a
pinstripe suit . . and leather gloves . . . And everyone was

talking to him in German. There was also a man they kept calling 'Doctor'.

First of all they gave me a cigarette, one of those with the filter tip, which I don't like too much, because they taste of straw, but I said thank you just the same, and no sooner had they lit it for me than they gave me a great slap, which sent the cigarette flying, and I started choking on the smoke. And I remembered my poor husband; at least before they shot him, they let him smoke his last cigarette almost down to the end.

'Now, talk, because it'll be best for you,' they told me.

I said: 'But I really don't know anything . . ' I should add that I was speaking in the dialect of my village, which none of them could understand, but there was a bastard of a Blackshirt there from Bagnacavallo, who began to translate for them what I was saying . . . And then I was also making out that I couldn't understand what the 'Doctor' was saying to me . because he was a Southerner (and I really was having a bit of difficulty . .). So they ended up having to translate for me too . . Anyway, they already knew everything about what I had been up to, and they spelled it all out: that I was a courier for Mario's Partisan Action Group, as well as being a nurse for the partisans, and that I had been here . . and there .

'But no,' I told them, still in dialect, 'I'm Dr Mario Bonora's housekeeper. Ask him, if you don't believe me.' The fact was that first they would have to catch Mario, if they wanted to ask him . . !

Anyway, then the man with the glasses and the pinstripe suit and the leather gloves got angry, and he punched me right in the face, on the nose, and started me bleeding . . I suppose he'd understood right away, without needing a translation, that time! Then they opened a door, and brought in one of the fellows who had been wounded, from the Seventh Brigade infirmary where I had been working. They had ripped off all his bandages, and he was black and blue, with his face all swollen, and you couldn't see his eyes for the swelling, and they asked him: 'Do you know this woman?' And they opened his eyes with their fingers . . . and he shook his head, to indicate that he didn't know me . . They took him away, pushing him and kicking him, and he didn't let out so much as a murmur!

Then they put a rope around my neck, and started hauling on it as if they were intending to hang me. 'Tell us the names of the doctors who work for the infirmary, and where they are,' they shouted. And as soon as they loosened the rope, I said: 'But I didn't know that those people who came to the doctor's house were partisans. If I had known, I would have reported them.'

At this point they pulled up my petticoat, and my dress, over my head, and with a knout they began to beat me on the belly, on the backside, and here, on my breasts, over and over again, as if I was an animal

By this time it was about seven o'clock, and they had all taken off their jackets, because they were sweating. They tipped a bucket of icy water over me .   I was lying in a heap on the floor, and blood was coming out of my mouth .   I was afraid that it was from my lungs, but it turned out it was because they had broken two of my teeth .   these ones here, you see   They're false

They pulled me up, and they sat me on a chair. I was completely naked, because they had torn all my clothes off me. They kept asking me questions, and there was a fellow there with a typewriter. I answered them, still in dialect, and with this business with the interpreter it was getting a bit drawn-out. So then the Doctor said: 'We're wasting our time here. Don't you see – the woman is plainly insane. She's crazy   . If she knew anything, she would have talked by now.' And he pulled the sheet of paper out of the typewriter and ripped it up.

'Take her away.'

And they called: 'Antonietta'. A huge fat woman came in, who must have been this Antonietta, and she lifted me up bodily and carried me off to a windowless room, where there was a bed. The bed was completely filthy, but at that moment it felt like heaven on earth for me.

Anyway, half an hour passed, and all of a sudden the man with the pinstripe suit came in . . . Now he wanted to be with me . . Yes, that's right, after all the beatings he'd given me, he wanted . . . you know what I mean.

'But I cannot even give you a kiss,' I said, politely, 'My whole mouth is broken up, with two teeth smashed out . .'

But he came over close to me, to touch my body and kiss me . . . I couldn't even move. I was all broken up . . . And I asked him: 'Have you no pity . . . ? Imagine, if I was one of your daughters, in this condition.' But it was like talking to an animal   !

When he went away, I started crying my heart out .   crying more than I'd even cried when I thought they were about to hang me . . This time I really did want to die . . and how I wept .   . Then I heard somebody calling me. Calling me with my real name. 'Luisa, Luisa.' I turned my head upwards, and there was a little window, and I saw the head of that young lad whose bandages they had ripped off, and who had said that he didn't recognise me .   'What are you doing there?'

'Well, I'm locked up in here,' he said .

'You been here long?'

'Yes, for ages . . . But if the reason that you're crying is because of what that pig did to you . . . don't get upset . . They'll pay for that too!'

I made a big effort, and I hauled myself up, so that I could get close to him, and I saw the state of his face . . . His eyes were swollen up like eggs .   . and there was blood coming out of them.

There was a wash basin in there . . I got down off the bed
. . . I walked across, clinging to the wall .   There was a
little towel hanging there too . . . I put it under the tap .
He realised that I wanted to bathe his eyes, and he said:
'Don't worry about me, look after yourself. You're half
dead yourself   '

But then, as I washed away his blood, he said: 'Thanks a
lot, that feels good .   And now I can even see a bit.'

Then it suddenly struck me that I was completely naked.
But it really didn't matter at all; I didn't even move my
hands to cover myself.

'I'm up for the firing squad tomorrow,' he said, 'But don't
worry, you'll be all right . . My only regret is that I won't
be there, on the day of the Liberation, to see it .   . It will
be a wonderful day   . But the best will be still to come.
Afterwards   '

'Afterwards? When?' I asked .   And then he said, as if he
was angry: 'But Luisa, why do you think that we're here,
getting ourselves killed, and letting ourselves be beaten like
dogs? It's for *afterwards*, don't you see   . ? For what
happens afterwards, when we'll really be free! Then we'll
have communism for real . . . just like in Russia .   We'll
build it ourselves .   . But it's not going to be easy at all .
Hey, how I'd love to be around to see it . . . And there's
still going to be battles that'll have to be fought, because the
boss class is hardly going to say: "Come on in, make
yourselves at home" .   They'll move heaven and earth to
stop us . . . But this time, Luisa, we shall have guns. *Our*
guns . . And we'll be playing another tune . .   This time
"Revolution, Revolution is going to win .   ".'

And he began to sing . . . Then, the morning after, while it
was still dark, they shot him.

As for me, they put me in the San Giovanni-in-Monte
mental hospital, because they decided that I really was mad
. . Then, when the day of the Liberation came, I was
released .   . What a wonderful day that was! But that

young lad they had executed was right . . . I didn't even know his name . . . It's not at all easy to build communism, because the bosses don't tell us: 'Please, make yourselves at home . . .' But I'm still hopeful, because otherwise, otherwise why would I still be a communist?'

translated by ED EMERY

The Eel-Woman

In the following account, a woman from the valleys between Comacchio and Chioggia, near the mouth of the River Po, tells us of the birth of a resistance group which was organised by communists, and which consisted solely of communists. All we know of her is her nom de guerre *from the partisan period: 'Risola'. In the original, the woman speaks in dialect: Chioggia dialect, a dialect from which, so they say, both the Venetian and Ferrarese dialects originated.*

The account is taken from a tape recording which the woman made after the War.

*   *   *

CHORUS: Avii! Sareee! Avi-avii-Mori-mori
Taij Taij . . . iiee Sare'ee!
Our life is down in the valley
Catching eels, salting them and smoking them,
And our love is down there in the valley,
Cuddling the girls, entwined like eels.
Avii! Sareee! Avi-avii-Mori-mori,
Taij! Taij . . . iiee Sare'ee!
And the eels are our soup
And the eels are our bread,
Even when we're dead, they bury us in water
Down among the wet ropes and the rotting eels.
Avii! Sareee! Avi-avii-Mori-mori
Taij! Taij . . . iiee Sare'ee!

ACTRESS: In early October in 1943, we were down at the sheds of Maria Negra, down on the lower island, all of us, working: men, women, children .   We were cutting the heads off the eels, so that then we could smoke them and dry them. We were out there in the courtyard, cutting with our big knives, and all of a sudden we saw a little boat coming across the water, with an army captain on board. You could see straight away that he was a landlubber: every time the boatman gave a sweep of his oar, he lost his balance, as if he was drunk.

We spotted that captain when he was still a good way off, as small as an ant, and then he came closer and closer, and slowly got bigger. We had been expecting him for a while . . We had heard that he was going round all the islands and the eel-sheds looking for men to go with him to act as scouts, to lead him and his rebels, with their boats. That was why, when he landed, no one even looked at him, not even the children. Nobody greeted him, even . . . He told us that he was even willing to pay us, and that the English were giving him money . . . Anyway, he talked on, and we just carried on cutting the heads off our eels: 'Scrunch, scrunch'. And we watched the eels writhing just the same way that that captain's tongue was writhing in his mouth . . He was spitting, but he carried on speaking: 'Take up arms with us!' he said. 'For the motherland, against the German invader. Liberate our sacred soil from the foreigner . .' and so on. A string of fancy words, just like the ones that the kids have printed on their books at school.

My father let him say his piece, and then he answered. And as he began to speak, everybody stopped cutting the heads off their eels, and everybody listened.

'Mr Captain, I served in the 1915–18 war,' he said. 'Out of twenty-two of us who left this valley to go and fight, and to chase out the invader, as you put it, only three of us ever came back. But when we came back, we discovered that the real invader was right here, in our valleys, in our houses . . . The bosses of the fishing reserves, which before had been common; they'd bought up everything, land and water alike, and we were left high and dry! So now, Mr Captain, you can stop trying to treat us like simpletons! You want us to go through that butchery yet again, so as to chase out the Germans and bring in the English? But what difference will it make for us, if the bosses are still there when we get back?'

'But you can't argue like that,' shouted the Captain. 'That's a self-centred, egoistic point of view . . How can you stand there, impassive and indifferent, faced with these criminals, these Fascists?'

'Oh, Mr Captain!' my father said. 'But who was it who set up these Fascists? Hasn't it always been these bosses of ours who set up the Fascist squads who came down to beat us during our strikes . . . ? The same people who are running the army in which you are now a captain
    ? And now that you don't get on with them any more, you come to ask us to liberate you from them!'

And everyone was so pleased with these words, that all of us started cutting the heads off our eels again, and there was a tremendous racket . . And the eels writhed and squealed, as if they were enjoying his words too. And the Captain went away . . angry, and cursing under his breath. He was saying some pretty terrible things: 'Animals . . . fishermen . . . smuggler mentality .   !' And he lurched about on the boat, losing his balance, even worse than when he arrived!

Two days later, another fellow turned up, who was neither a captain nor even a soldier . . . He was wearing civilian clothes, and his face was pale, white . . . He spoke quietly, never raising his voice. The boatman who turned up with him, who rowed him over, was someone I knew well: it was Togno de la Rosa . . . a gamekeeper, a good man, and a communist. I liked him, that Togno . We were friends, even though he had tried to shoot my brother one time when he was poaching eels from the fishing reserve.

Togno immediately explained who this fellow was who was speaking so gently. He told us that he'd come out of prison a little while previously: he'd served twelve years! He was a people's commissar . . . And this commissar was also asking our menfolk to go and serve as rebels.

'I have not even had time to see my wife and my daughters,' he said. 'They told me to come here immediately, to the valleys, to organise armed bands, because of the experience I have from the war in Spain We've got the men: stragglers, escaped prisoners of war, New Zealanders, Russians, deserters, Czechoslovaks, and so on. But if some of you don't come to lead us through all these reeds and marshes, we're going to be lost like babes in the wood . . . and at the first Fascist round-up, they'll catch us all   !'

'Why should we join your rebels?' answered my father. 'The English are going to win anyway, even without us You know that yourselves, don't you?'

'Yes, that's what I believe, yes,' said the commissar.

'All right then, so why don't we wait and let them get on with it, since they've got the aeroplanes .   the bombs, the big guns   ? And the cans of meat .   Let those English go out and get killed, and not us poor wretches, because afterwards we're still going to be poor wretches, whatever happens!'

At this point, the commissar raised his voice a bit: 'But it's precisely so as not to have to remain poor wretches that we're going to have to fight this battle .   take arms now, if we want to count for something afterwards, when the liberation comes!'

My father shook his head .   'Schoolbook words,' he muttered. 'Printed words . . . !'

Then Togno de la Rosa spoke up. 'First we'll chase out the Fascists and the Germans, and then we'll use the same guns to chase out the bosses! I wouldn't be here to

risk my skin if I wasn't convinced that one day I won't
have to shoot poachers any more . . . because we will all
be bosses of the eels and of the valley!'

Then there was a long silence . . . And when the two of
them got back in their boat, my brother Peo jumped into
his own boat, and went over to join them. My father
didn't say a word .   . My mother was crying quietly to
herself .

Ten days later, my brother Peo came back to the eel shed
of Maria Negra: he had his boat full of sacks .   . stuff
stolen from the warehouses in Argenta and Comacchio,
stuff that belonged to the landowners. And he left us .
oh, Holy Mary .   ! A sack of maize flour, a little sack
of salt and a half sack of sugar   .

And then he went over to the eel shed of the Franconis,
and then to the Manzers, and he took them some sacks of
stuff too. Then we heard that the owners of the
warehouses had got angry, and that before they had been
waiting for the English to liberate them, but now that
they had been stripped of some of their property, they
moved fast and asked for help from the Fascist
Blackshirts and the Germans, who began going looking
for rebels.

A couple of days later, there were some shots, and two
Germans ended up dead on the river bank near Filo. As a
result, the Germans carried out a reprisal massacre at
Filo: they put ten men up before the firing squad, as well
as Algide Cavalli, my mother's sister, who had kept
trying to push the Germans out of her house so as to give
her son time to escape . . . Even she was killed, poor
thing!

That day, my father got into his boat too, the last boat
remaining on the river bank. I went running down behind
him: 'Let me come with you, Dad, I can handle the oar
for you!'

He didn't want me to: 'No, there's no place for girls in this business . . It's war . . It's very dangerous.'

'But what if the Germans turn up and burn down our houses and kill us, like they did at Filo? Isn't that dangerous too?' And I went off with my father to join the armed band which was staying in the Codigoro Valley, in the eel fishers' huts.

Their leader was a man called Manazza, from Mulino. No sooner did I arrive than my father wanted to send me back, because the men all started undressing me with their eyes, because I was eighteen then, and breaking out fore and aft! I stayed, though. They used to send me round, down to Borgo Caprile, Riva, Ostellato and so on, to see what the Germans and the Fascists were doing . . . I also served as a courier, bringing orders for the Gordini band, down in the Argenta valleys . . and I also used to bring stuff to eat. There wasn't a lot to eat, and the weapons were even fewer . . . Out of the ninety people in our band, only half of them had rifles, and they only had thirty bullets apiece. We were expecting an airdrop, but it never arrived, because the English don't willingly hand out arms to communists.

One day I was coming back from the house of the Balladora family, where the Garavini detachment was billeted, and behind the Travego wood I saw four Blackshirts coming towards me . . They pulled me down off my bicycle, and began touching me and groping me . . and I didn't want them touching me, because in my knickers I had hidden the maps showing the gun emplacements, which they'd given me, so as to pass them on to Manazza. So I started crying, and telling them that I was engaged to a German from the Ostellato command, and that if he found out that they'd laid hands on me, he'd kill the lot of them.

The Blackshirts suddenly went pale, and went off, and didn't even turn round to look back . . . But that evening I was so trembling with fright that no sooner did I arrive

at the eel fishers' hut than I flung myself into the arms of
Nane the Red, crying my heart out . . . He gave me a big
strong hug . . . He was very good-looking, that Nane . .
And I liked having him hug me like that . . And so the
emotion made me cry even more .

In among the maps that I had hidden in my knickers,
there was a letter telling us that an English captain was
due to arrive in order to inspect us to see whether they
could send us arms. Orders were given to get rid of all the
red flags and the red kerchiefs that we wore around our
necks, all the men to cut their hair and shave their
beards, to clean ourselves up, and to set up a Committee
of National Liberation. What this meant was that in our
command group, as well as having a communist, we also
had to have a republican, a socialist, a Christian
Democrat, a liberal, and if possible, even a monarchist
. . But we didn't have any people like that in our
band . .   We were all reds, and that was that!

So, Manazza said: 'You, Greco, from this moment on
you're going to be a republican. You, Anguilla, you can
be the socialist, and you, Bagnoli, you'll be the Action
Party!' But nobody, I mean nobody, wanted to be the
Christian Democrat, and so we did without!

So everybody started patching up their clothes .
shaving their beards and cutting their hair, and putting
tricolour rosettes all over the place, so that soon we
looked more like a bunch of Bersaglieri than partisans!
As for me, they sent me to the priest's house, at Borgo
Caprile, to tell the parish priest, who was called Don
Ragano, to come to the huts at once, as quickly as he
could, because Nane the Red was dying and wanted
confession so that he could die as a Christian.

Don Ragano was not very happy about having to come,
and didn't want to budge. But in the end he came,
because I told him that if he didn't, Manazza and my
brother would come to get him anyway, and they were a

pretty mean pair. And so it was that Don Ragano came to serve as our chaplain for two days.

And the fact that we had a chaplain, as well as tricolour rosettes and haircuts, made a very good impression on the English inspectors who arrived . . . so that they sent us two or three tons of weapons, on big naval motorboats, which came from Pescara. Ah yes, now we began to give the Fascists and the Germans a run for their money . . No barracks or Fascist's house was safe any more. Every night one of them would be blown sky-high! And within a month they didn't find it so easy to go down the Romea road either!

During that period, we were expecting the English to break through the German front, which was not very far off . . . It was just behind Rimini . . But no, Alexander, the English general, sent a message to tell us that they weren't in a hurry . and that they would break through the German lines next year, in spring, and that for the moment they couldn't . . You see ?! They didn't want to ! And what about us poor devils, where were we supposed to spend the winter? With all the valleys flooded and icing over? Maybe we were supposed to go to the seaside? 'Go back to your houses,' Alexander told us . just like that . 'Dissolve your bands, and go back to your homes.'

'You swine . . . ! What do you mean – back to our homes . ? We're already in our homes . . and with the Germans going around squashing us like eels, if we split up our band, they'll be able to pick us off more easily, one by one . . No, Alexander can go to hell . We're all going to stay down here in the valley . united!'

And the Germans began combing the valleys with their big motor boats full of soldiers armed with machine guns as big as cannons. And there were lots of these big boats. They closed in to flush us out. That was how they took all the partisans in the Bendo group, who were living in the

Manzers' eel shed . . . They killed all of them, including
the Manzers' old grandmother, a child, and a dog!

'See here, if we don't make the first move, we're as good
as dead,' we thought. And so it happened that all the
armed bands decided to meet together at Valle di
Mulino. There were about two hundred of us . . . We had
waited for a day when there was a lot of wind, blowing
large waves right up the valleys . . And as the Germans
were going down the Mezzan Canal, changing the guards
on the bridges, our lads, up on the Franconis' island,
which is at the top of the waterway, began firing on them
with a mortar. This was like telling the Germans: 'Come
and get us!' And the Germans came . There were
eight motor boats . . They came out from the canals .
They spaced themselves out over a broad front, as per
usual .   And off they went   ! But this time it was
not so easy .   There were large waves breaking in their
faces, breaking up against their boats, and those
particular boats had flat bottoms, and the waves caught
them sideways on, and set them dancing

We let them dance for a while, and then, out of the reeds
which were all around, all our boats came .   Lots of
them .   a real lot   ! There must have been about
forty   . cutting through the waves at speed, because
they were so slender. And I was in my brother Peo's
boat, sweeping with the oar like a mad woman .   And
everyone was singing and shouting like we do when we go
in for the kill with the tuna fish: 'Andiamo! Avanti!
Forza! Serrate   !'

All of a sudden all the waters of the valley were full of
fast-moving black boats, and there was a lot of shouting,
and the sound of shots .   . And the Germans were
bouncing about, and weren't able to take aim .   . with
the waves that were knocking them all over the place.
And our lads were firing accurately, sprawled out in the
bows of their boats, hidden down in the waves, which
were pierced with each sweep of the oar. And they were

all shouting: 'Ahii .   . Aprite .   . Serrate .   . Avanti
    Tagliate .   Tagliate   '

The Germans were under a hail of grenades and bullets
from all sides . . . They were just about out for the count
    . And when the motor boats were hit front-on, they
turned over, and down they went, with machine guns,
men and all, drowned .   'Ahii .   . Serrate .   . Avanti
    Tagliate .   Tagliate .   !'

Then the English came. Then the Canadians. Then the
Americans. Then all of them went away, and all that was
left was us . . . and the bosses .   . Us, down at Maria
Negra's eel shed, cutting the heads off our eels just like
before .   . eels in your soup, eels with your bread . . .
And every year some fellow comes from Rome to put a
wreath on the monument at Filo. A general . .   They
make speeches, and everyone stands to attention, and I
remember my father, and the way he always used to say:
'Schoolbook words .   . Printed words . . .'

translated by ED EMERY

Mamma Togni

'Mamma Togni . . . Mamma Togni, the Fascists are in the streets at Monte Beccaria; they want to hold a public meeting in the square!'

Two young lads from downstairs came up to call me .

'Who's going to be talking? Who's the Fascist?'

'Servello.'

'That bastard! Let's go . . . let's go! Wait while I get my stick, though .   . I've got a swollen ankle, I'll need it.'

Now I see why those two party comrades called round earlier. They wanted to be sure that nobody had been round to tell me .   . They tell me: 'You're old, don't get involved . . . Something might happen to you . . . But most of all, don't let people try to make use of you. Stay at home . . . Don't get involved.' But I say that when it comes to Fascists, I'm never too old! So let's go. And what's all this nonsense about not letting myself be used? Against the Fascists? Those blackshirt bastards who have the nerve to come and make their vile speeches in the same square where they killed fourteen of our kids right before their mothers' eyes? Come on, let's go!!

When I arrived up at the main square, there was a handful of people hanging round the platform, and carabinieri all over the place. I told the lads who were with me: 'You stay here, don't you dare move.'

'No, Mamma Togni. We're coming with you.'

'No, you shut up and stay there. Otherwise I'm going back. I'll go on my own, because they won't dare touch me.'

So I hobbled over with my stick .   And I made my way to the platform .

'Excuse me, excuse me .   .' Up on the platform, wrapped round the microphone so tightly that he looked like he was trying to eat it, was that bastard Servello, and he was shouting and waving his arms around like a policeman in the rush hour.

I gave the mike stand a whack with my stick, so that the microphone almost smashed his teeth, and then I started singing:

> 'You blackshirt bastards,
> You came to kill us yesterday,
> And now here you are again!'

For a moment, Servello stopped bawling down the microphone, and he looked at me. Then he carried on with his speech. So I started singing again, and he lost his thread. From the back of the square, under the arcades, the lads started singing too! Then I lifted my stick and gave him a good whack, right on the knee, which had him yowling like a scalded cat!

At this point, the captain of the carabinieri comes over to me, takes me by the arm, and says: 'Excuse me, madam, what on earth do you think you're doing? I could have you arrested for breach of the peace, you know, because you're disturbing a public meeting.'

'On the contrary, my dear lieutenant,' (I decided to downgrade him a couple of ranks.) 'It's the public meeting which is disturbing me, because these characters are the self-same murderers who came here and gunned down our kids like dogs, even though they hadn't done anything . As a reprisal . . .'

'That's as maybe .   . But now they have official permission to speak .   .'

'Permission from whom? From the mothers of the young people they shot? Hey, come on, you mothers of Monte Beccaria! Did they ask *your* permission to come and put on this disgusting display? I'm talking to you! Come out from under the arches . . Come and tell him what happened.'

'Please, madam, will you stop that, because otherwise I shall be obliged to have you removed.'

'Oh yes? You so much as lay a hand on me, and I'll faint. I'm telling you . . And then you're going to need at least ten men to lift me, because I weigh a good ninety kilos! Don't say I didn't warn you!'

'Well,' said the captain, 'well, if it comes to that, I have seventy men at my disposal.'

'Seventy men? Wonderful! You need seventy men to protect this dirty murderous bastard, so's he can speak here? The fact is that *honest* people in this town don't need police protection if they want to make speeches in public

We communists can make speeches here at any time of day or night, and we don't need police to guard us! The fact is that you're forcing this shithead Servello down our throats.'

'You mustn't call him that. He's a senator.'

'A senator? A senator of our Republic that was created by the Resistance? Ha! Ladies and gentlemen, did you hear that? Is this what our sons and our husbands were killed for? Is this why they died for the Liberation of Italy? So as to bring us a republic with a Senate where these sons of bitches can go and start spreading their filth again?'

'Now that's enough, madam. I shall be forced to remove you.'

'No. If you are an honest man, you remove that bastard there, because if you don't, then I will, with my stick. Because you might have hearts and guts like soggy semolina
 . I'm talking to you, men and women of Monte Beccaria
 . but I'm not prepared to stand here and let them insult

the memory of my son, whom they killed, as if it was yesterday, and my husband who died in 1923, when these fascists beat him and beat him till he ended up coughing his own lungs up . . .'

By now I was shouting so much that I hardly knew what I was saying. Anyway, from the back of the square, two or three men started to move forwards, and a few women, and the lads too, even though I'd told them to stay where they were. At that point the carabinieri suddenly went mad . . They started charging the kids, and beating them down in some kind of blind fury. And there was the captain, with two of his men, pushing me away, because by now there was such confusion that they thought they could get away with it, and they gave me bruises on my shoulders and my back which I still have to this moment . . . But at the time I didn't even feel them . . . I was worried for the lads. I was shouting: 'Stop it!! You scum!! Why pick on them? What have they done? Leave them alone, you Nazis! Fascists!'

Three or four of the young people had ended up on the ground with bleeding heads, and the police were still kicking hell out of them. Then they tossed eleven of them into the police wagon.

'Where are they taking the kids . . ? Down to the police station . . . Somebody get a car . . Take me to the police station at once . . . And you others, go and contact one of our lawyers . . .'

I arrived at the police station, and went up, together with one of our Party members, a town councillor, to try to convince the constable at the door to let me talk with his Chief, or with anyone, so as to explain our side of what had happened.

All of a sudden the constable pretended that somebody had punched him, and he dived to the ground. As if he'd been knocked unconscious! I was no more than three feet away from the man, and I swear nobody had touched him. But all of a sudden, about fifty carabinieri dived on us, and they beat our councillor around the head so badly that blood was flowing everywhere . . . I started shouting: 'You bastards – you've set this up deliberately . . . Murderers . . . Fascists!'

So they grabbed hold of me, bundled me up, and carried me off inside. I was to be charged straight away.

While they were taking down my details, I could hear voices out in the street – all our comrades, shouting: 'Free Mamma Togni . . . Free Mamma Togni . . . !' It was lovely to hear them. I felt so good that I would happily have signed up to get arrested every day! Anyway, at this point the superintendent came in, and he didn't notice that I was there, because I was hidden by the door. He was shouting: 'What silly bastard decided to lock up the Togni woman? What on earth were you thinking of? There'd have been less of a fuss if you'd arrested the President of the Republic in person!!' And I began singing to myself, casually:

'You blackshirt bastards,
You came to kill us yesterday,
And now here you are again!'

They all went very quiet, and more or less tiptoed out of the room because they couldn't face staying there. The only one who stayed was a young constable, who looked at me with a sort of half smile, as if he was embarrassed.

'I've heard all about you, signora,' he said, 'because my dad was a commander during the Resistance, in the Liguria mountains.'

'Was he in Lazagna's division?'

'Yes.'

'And what was your father's name?'

'Mirko .   . Mirko was his battle name.'

'But Mirko's dead. They shot him . . . !'

'Yes, that's right . . . I was only three when they killed him.'

'He was a good man, Mirko. Your father was a good partisan . . . And now you've joined the carabinieri? Well done, son! You've joined the boss class!'

He lowered his eyes, and turned pale . . . Or maybe that's just the way it seemed, because carabinieri always look pale, to me. Anyway, the trial was a farce. The judge's main concern was to get me out of the way, so that he could lay the blame on the kids and lock them away. It was completely ludicrous.

'Madam, I am sure that you were only there in the square by accident . . weren't you? You happened to be passing . And anyway,' (*He was trying to help me, here, putting words into my mouth.*) 'when your stick hit the microphone, and the senator's knee, it was an accident, wasn't it   ?'

'It wasn't an accident at all! I did it deliberately. I'd have hit him over the head too, if I'd had the chance, and what's more, the next time that pig of a fascist comes, I'll break his head open.'

'I must ask you not to talk like that   I realise that you're rather upset   '

'Not a bit of it. I'm very calm and relaxed.'

'No, you are upset. In the same way that you were obviously upset when you started calling the police pigs and fascists, and so ended up exciting these young hooligans!'

'No. To start with, the real troublemakers were the police, and not the young people. What's more those police have a very strange way of arresting people   . kicking them and booting them in the head as if they're playing football   !'

'All right   . But you do realise that it's against the law to shout things like "Fascists" and "Pigs"?'

'Of course I realise . . . But in the old days when we were up in the mountains, those of us who ended up against a wall died in the belief that after the Liberation those who were killing them would no longer be around . . . But far from it. Here they all are, in charge of the riot police. I called them fascist swine then, and I call them swine and fascists now!'

The judge turned pale . . . He didn't know what to say . but I had realised that the only way to get our people off the hook was for me to go in as hard as I could. Obviously they wouldn't dare sentence me, because they would end up looking stupid. So they had to abandon the trial, and let them all go free . . . At least for the moment.

What a party it was when we came out. Everybody was there, all the comrades, and we were all kissing and hugging and singing. It was 'Mamma Togni' here, 'Mamma Togni' there . . . and people taking me by the arm, and greeting me with clenched fists. It was wonderful. Like a big party . Like the Liberation all over again! What a shame that my boy wasn't there to see it. 'Mum,' he'd said, 'if for any reason I don't come back, you must stay with the comrades until it's over, you hold out with them.'

'Yes, son, I will '

'And how could I possibly have left them? I was a nurse, I'd done my exams, and, without wanting to boast, I was good. I had upwards of fifty wounded men that I was looking after in the sanatorium. I remember when the Germans came round on their raids . . . People were trying to persuade me to lie low . . . they'd found me a job in a hospital . . . but I'd rather have died . . I took my thirty-two wounded lads, and we hobbled off . The ones who were limping were helping the ones who couldn't see; and one who had a stomach wound was being carried on a stretcher by two others who had bandages round their heads . . We looked like a gang of desperadoes, but we went on, and I actually managed to save them. I saved all of them. The real problem was finding enough food every day, enough for thirty-two men to be able to eat, day after day . . . So I would leave them in a barn somewhere, or under a bridge, and I set off searching for food. House to house. And everywhere, even though they had almost nothing left, these peasants, these mountain people, were still willing to take the food out of their own mouths in order to help us . . They tore up their sheets too, to give me bandages for the wounded. Their best bed linen, even . . . But on occasion it happened that I went to ask for help from well-to-do families, in the towns, and they used to say, 'No, we can't give you anything.' So I would suddenly pull out my P38 pistol, with its fifteen rounds, and I would stick it under their noses and shout: 'All right. Seeing that you're so mean, now you're going to give me everything I'm asking for, because otherwise I'm going to kill you. Shame on you – because these boys are dying for you too!'

So, you see, I even went robbing to save my lads. Does anyone object? Because I can tell you, I would do the same again today. My lads . . . I was a mother to them . . . Mamma Togni, they called me. God help anyone who laid a finger on Mamma Togni. They used to say: 'Nobody ever says No to Mamma Togni!'

And they all used to do what I told them!

On a spring day in 1944, my son was part of a group that went off to attack the barracks of the fascists. An hour later I saw Ciro coming back, white as a sheet. He said:

'They've wounded him. Your son's been wounded.'

'Stand there, Ciro. Look me in the eye. I won't cry. I won't scream . . . Just look me in the eye . . . He's dead, isn't he. I know he's dead.'

'Yes.'

Two of them carried him up to me, in their arms.

I sat myself down, and they put him on my knee. He had a little bullet hole here, in his neck. Then the comrades took him away for me . . . They took him off, and I went inside, into the big room where all my wounded lads were. I told them: 'Listen, boys, my son's been killed. Now I no longer have anyone to call me mother . . . And I . . . I need . . .'

There was a long silence, and then they all shouted: 'You're our mum!' And they were calling me 'Mamma', with tears in their eyes.

And so it was that everyone came to know me as Mamma Togni. And don't let them come telling me: 'You're too old, don't go getting involved .   you've already done your bit.'

No, for as long as these murderers are around, these fascists, we have to go out in the streets, and tell the young people what we know. We have to tell them what happened in the old days, up in the mountains, because that way they will learn. No, don't let them come telling me to stay at home because I'm too old. You're only too old when you decide that you'd rather stay at home with your feet in front of the fire just like they want you to.

At that point you're old .   In fact you're as good as dead!

translated by ED EMERY

Fascism 1922

It was 1922. I was still a girl, a young thing, twelve or thirteen . That was the year you first started in the factory . and I could already see the Fascists in operation . Because, during a strike, they came to take away people in the union, including a man called Frigiani, my cousin . . and they beat him senseless, and the police were there, and they never said a word . they just looked away, as if nothing was happening . Then they killed one of the Party members from the Oleggio branch; smashed him round the face and damaged his eyesight, so that he ended up going blind, and then he suffered a stroke, and shortly afterwards he died.

As a result, the men in the Party, which included the menfolk of my family, went to the Chamber of Labour, to protest that they'd had enough. They spoke with someone who turned out to be Matteotti, and they said: 'This has gone far enough! We must organise ourselves, to do something about it!'

And Ramella was there, at the Chamber of Labour, the Member of Parliament, who had been good in his time, and who was still capable of firing off the occasional salvo, but, as my father used to say, he was all words and no action, because Ramella was a reformist at heart.

So when the men and the women of our Party branch, in other words more or less everyone in the village, went to complain about what was happening with the Fascists, he answered us in the same way as when he made his speeches from the balcony of the Chamber of Labour . . He used to

come out on the balcony, and he would always say: 'Keep
calm, and don't get over-excited .   . Calm and peaceful
    You'll see, they'll go away   '

And one of our number, who was a railway worker,
shouted back: 'Don't be so stupid . . . What do you mean,
"they'll go away"? Huh! Where to? *We're* the ones who will
have to go away, with leaders like you .   . Get off with you
– you're a traitor   That's what you are!'

And someone shouted: 'What do you know about anything
– you're just a stoker'. And Ramella said: 'Let him say his
bit   because he doesn't know what he's talking about!'

The Party members went to the Federation office to protest:
'What are we supposed to do? Should we take sticks and
beat them, too?' And he said: 'No, no, just because they're
evil, that's no reason why you should be the same. Instead
of blood being spilled just once, it'll be spilled twice. Leave
them alone   Keep calm.'

But he knew that this business about 'keeping calm' wasn't
on. We *had* to find a way to defend ourselves, because they
were even coming to get us in our houses   ! And what
were we supposed to do   .   ? Just stay there and take a
kicking? Just keep quiet about it? This was the way it
always was: forcing our people to drink castor oil, beating
them with sticks and clubs . . . and every now and then a
bullet in your guts! We should have organised ourselves
from the start! If we'd been organised from the start, they'd
never have been able to get away with treating us like that
     . No, they would never have been able to crush us the
way they did. But all he ever said was: 'Keep calm, keep
calm .   Don't get over-excited.'

Oh to hell with him! When the Fascists arrived at the
Chamber of Labour with their guns, we had no guns
ourselves. We only had sticks and stones .   And no guns,
because Ramella didn't want it.
    'If those Fascists find out that we've got guns,' he said,

'that will give them even more reason to attack us. I am against bloodshed!'

'Well said!' my father told him. 'So the only ones who end up shedding their blood will be us!' And then somebody else spoke up: 'If you're against bloodshed, how are you ever going to make a revolution? How are you ever going to get the proletariat into power? By reforms .   ? Because in that case, you'll be waiting till the cows come home!'

By that time, in our branch almost everybody was communist, after the Livorno split. Everybody was saying that if we didn't have guns in our hands, then we were done for .

One day   . I must have been twelve or thirteen, as I said . . . I was there, in the club, washing glasses in the main hall, all on my own .   . And about ten of these Fascists suddenly arrived at the door . . . They came in, and stopped in front of this picture of an old man . . . One of them looked up, and he said: 'Ha! There he is – the workers' friend!' And he takes a club, goes over to the picture, stands up on a chair, and smashes it into a thousand pieces. At that point .   . I was only young .   . I ran out, because I was scared . . . and I went to get my father, who was president of the club at the time .   . 'Dad, they've smashed the picture of Karl Marx .   .'

When they heard that, all the people came out of where they'd been playing cards. There were both communists and socialists together in the club at that time, even though there had already been the split in the Socialist Party . And they were all furiously angry . . . So they all went to the hall .   . But by that time the Fascists had already gone!

'If they've come once, it means they'll come again, for sure.' So everyone started collecting up rocks and stones, and bottles, and sticks, and prepared them in the clubhouse. But they didn't come back straightaway. Almost a month went by .

It was a fine day in June .   . And there they came again, with their bicycles. There must have been thirty or forty of them . . . And in front there was a red open-topped car, full of Fascists, flying the black flag . . . and they were all armed, some of them with two guns apiece .

I was in the clubhouse at the time, and the place was full of our comrades .   . All of a sudden a woman – it was Olla's mother – ran in, and she was shouting in a strange, thin sort of voice . . . 'They're coming! The Fascists are coming . And they've got guns   '

Everybody ran out into the street. 'Stick together, everyone. We'll show them!'

And we had the sticks and the stones, and the bottles . . . Full bottles, they were, so that they weighed more .   Full of water, of course, not wine!

Outside we set up a barricade .   'Look out, here they come!' My brother and the other young men went out and started throwing things at the Fascists as they came.
   One of those young men was a young communist from Sant'Agabio, and we saw him walk straight towards the Fascists' car, with a big stick in his hand . .   And the Fascists in the car fired at him, full in the face. Twice.

We heard a loud thud, and we saw blood coming out of the back of his head . . . And he didn't fall to the ground immediately . . . He was just standing there, as if in a trance . . . until one of the Fascists went and pushed him over.
   'Bastards! Murderers!!' our people shouted .   . And the Fascists went among the houses, and started shooting at people standing in the doorways .   Then, at a certain point, we saw Merlot come running out of one of the farm buildings, together with Caldani and his son. They were carrying pitchforks and mattocks . . . And they came running out so fast that the Fascists hardly had time to see them before they started smashing into the car with their forks and mattocks . .
   And two other shots went off .   . And we saw both of

them go down, both Caldani and Merlot .   They'd been wounded in the neck and chest .   .

Then the other members of the club came running. I remember it. As I say, I was twelve or thirteen, at the time .   . but I was in the thick of it, too. Running with my father, who was shouting at me: 'You stay out of this! Go home, at once!' And I shouted back: 'No, no!'   . And I saw our comrades go weighing into the Fascists, who were on their bicycles . . . And they were beating them on the backs with their sticks, which had them pedalling for dear life   And I saw one of them crash into a pillar, with his arms outstretched like a big fly on a window pane . . . ! And all of us, even the women . .   God, you should have seen the women   . With big forks, and shovels, and hoes   . Because none of us had guns, none of us   ! All we had was our worktools!

At this point the Fascists dumped their bicycles, and the red motor car too, and they ran off .   And we chased after them   . . so that they had to keep running until they reached Sant'Agabio .   And no sooner had they arrived in the village than they found other comrades, lying in wait for them .   . And they gave them another seeing to!

So we ended up with a pile of around thirty bicycles . And there, lying on the ground, our wounded .   There must have been thirty of us wounded .   . and six dead. Two of the dead were fathers of six or seven children . Another three, who had stomach wounds, died later on. Out of the Fascists, three died right there, on the spot, and one in hospital   .

In the evening, the carabinieri arrived, and they arrested nearly all of us .   The whole village   Not me, because I wasn't even thirteen yet   for 'riotous behaviour and multiple homicide'.

'What are you talking about? They attacked us first,' people were shouting. 'They started the killing first .   And they had guns! We were just trying to defend ourselves.'

'That's enough. The law is the law.'

They only arrested the communists. Not a single Fascist went inside.

But when it came to the time for the trial, they didn't dare carry it through . . . There never was a trial, because it was too dangerous for them .   They were determined not to let the word get out, because otherwise people everywhere would have found out how a small village of peasants, without guns, but just with their anger and courage, had united to chase out the Fascists .   . And they couldn't allow that . . . they couldn't allow it because it would have been a dangerous example for the rest of the country ˉ   . So they decided to keep quiet .   . and not do a thing!

translated by ED EMERY

An Arab Woman Speaks

At the start of the 1970s, Dario Fo and Franca Rame decided to put on a show dedicated to the Palestinian resistance. It was called Fedayeen. *This involved Franca Rame travelling to Lebanon to visit a refugee camp. The organisers of the camp had brought together around a hundred people. 'Our idea,' says Franca Rame, 'was that we would choose about a dozen young people, who would come to Italy to be part of the show, performing songs and recitations. They were to be the principal performers in this show, and we would have toured the whole of Italy, performing in upwards of a hundred locations.*

'I listened to a lot of people in the camp, but, curiously, none of them were women. Even though there were many women present in that tent.

'Some of the women had babes in arms, others were extremely young, and I had been told that many of them were stupendous singers. I asked whether it would be possible to invite one of them over to Italy, for the show. "Quite impossible," they replied. "The girls are doing a great job in this period. And leaving aside the organisational problems, there's another problem which is a bit hard to explain."

"Am I right in thinking that, despite all your talk about women's liberation, when it comes to the crunch you're not prepared to let your women go?" I asked one of the camp officials. "And you prefer to keep them shut away, hidden out of sight?"

"Perhaps you're right," he replied. "For us the problem of women's liberation is probably the biggest hurdle that we'll have to overcome."

'Sitting nearby was a woman who had a baby in her arms. She looked tired. When I asked her to tell me

something about herself, she shook her head, as if to say that she had nothing to tell.

'A short while after I returned to Milan, a comrade from Beirut sent me a tape. It was a recording of a woman's voice, speaking in Arabic. I had the tape transcribed and translated, and this is what she had to say.'

*   *   *

'I am the comrade who didn't reply to your question at the camp. Now I can tell you about myself. I am Bedouin by origin, from the Monchem tribe. My mother lived for many years in tents, like all the nomads, moving the length and breadth of the Jordan valley. She fell in love with a peasant, married him, and so it was that I came to be born between four walls, in a stone-built hut. I hated the work of a peasant woman .   What kind of a life was that? Dying of fatigue, like animals, always hungry for bread, hungry for sleep. And women were always bottom of the whole pile: always bent double. Bent over to weed the fields and gather in the harvest, bent over the well to fetch water, bent over the washing, bent to knead the dough for bread, bent before the priests, before the bosses, before their own husbands, even bent over their children, as they breast-fed them and helped them to take their first steps.

'My mother had been a fine figure of a woman when she was young, but now her skin was so cracked and withered that she looked like a piece of clay.

'Every now and then she would sigh as she remembered the days of her life as a nomad. She would tell me that the men used to treat their women like queens, and they would always make sure that they didn't work too hard, because work makes you old and ugly before your time. "They used to prevent us from carrying too heavy loads," she used to say. "And we used to wear light clothes, so that the wind could ruffle them and keep us cool. Our role in life was to sing well, and to dance better. To laugh pleasantly and to talk of things that were not too serious. A woman should never appear too intelligent."

'But one day a caravan of bedouins stopped near our camp, and I saw these famous "queens". Poor women, they were, all dressed in rags, with a gaggle of children around them, and obviously living a wretched life. I suppose you could say that my mother had a strong imagination, but I went way beyond her. I never missed a chance to play the part of the Bedouin queen. I was still a little girl, but I could ride a horse better than any Bedouin. I used to wear the transparent veil of my mother's tribe, and I would use white make-up on my face. Everyone took me for a lunatic. I used to go to school in a nearby village, because I enjoyed studying, and I was fairly clever. I got as far as the sixth grade. I hated working in the fields. I would have turned my hand to absolutely any job at all, just to escape that animal life. But my fate was that I ended up marrying a peasant. He had a bit of money, but he was still a peasant.

'I was sixteen years old at the time, and one Sunday there was a big celebration in the local square. Horseriders had come from outside, and they were performing fancy tricks on horseback. There was one man, dressed all in black, who stood on his horse's neck as he rode round, and fired into the air with a silver-embossed rifle. "That's the man for me," I thought. And I ended up marrying him. I'll spare you the details of all the little tricks I used to get him to marry me. He was strong, and really handsome, but as far as culture went, he was a disaster. The only thing that interested him was his silver rifle, his horse, and doing tricks on horseback. We married in his village. I arrived on my horse. He had given me the horse in place of an engagement ring; it was my engagement horse. All the relations greeted each other, in the customary fashion, and then the wedding celebrations began. They began with the dancing. I used to love dancing. All the men were asking me to dance. Then the stamping game began. The husband has to try to stamp on his wife's foot, as a sign that he has imposed his authority over her. It was a game, or so I thought, but I suddenly noticed that my husband was putting a lot of effort into it. His family were looking strangely tense, too. I managed to keep ducking out of his way, but in the end he gave me a big push, and then, bang, he stamped on my foot. I reacted immediately. I kicked him back. Hard. All the guests burst out laughing, but not his relations. They didn't laugh at all. "Well," I thought, "I see they have no sense of humour here." And I thought no more of it.

'I had heard my mother tell that in many of the villages of the interior they had the custom that the husband was supposed to beat his wife on the wedding night, before they made love. The idea of beating her was so that she got it firmly into her head that he, the man, was the boss, and that this was the treatment she could expect whenever she stepped out of line. I never suspected that this custom was still applied in my husband's village. But I did notice that, as we were going up into the bedroom, he seemed a bit embarrassed. When we were on our own, he said, "You know, I'm supposed to beat you now. But don't worry, I won't beat you very hard. All you have to do is start shouting and crying, so that they can hear you from downstairs."

'"What?" I said. "Are you crazy? You lay one hand on me, and I'll break this copper pot over your head."

'"Try to understand! These are our customs. I *have* to beat you. My dignity in the village is at stake."

'"To hell with your dignity. You're a bunch of cavemen here, and if you so much as touch me, I'll kill you!" So saying, I picked up the copper pot, ready to throw it at his head. And at this point, he burst out crying. ". . . You mustn't show me up like this." By now he was pleading. "Please, just do it for me. All you have to do is shout a bit and cry a bit, and I can bang on the mattress, like this . . ."

'"No. If you want, *I'll* bang on the mattress, and *you* can do the crying. Go on, start screaming!"

'And so saying, I pulled aside the bed cover. There I saw a large linen sheet, half a bedsheet, spread across the bed.

'"What's that for?"

'"It's for the show."

'"What 'show'?"

'"Tomorrow morning this sheet has to be hung out of the window, to show that it's bloodstained, so as to show the whole village that you were a virgin."

'I couldn't stop myself. I threw the copper pot at him. It hit him on the head. He let out a yell, and blood started pouring from his forehead .   Then I tore off the linen sheet and shouted: "There you go, make the most of it. Put *your* blood on it, you stupid man!"

'At this point, his mother came in. A terrible woman, short and fat, and I'd never seen her smile since the day I arrived there.

'"Why are you taking so long? Why haven't you beaten her?"

'"She won't let me."

'"In that case, I'll send your brothers up, and they'll beat you, and I'll tell them to throw you out. I'm not having a man with no balls living in this house."

'At this point my husband began shouting like a lunatic, and he leapt up and started beating me as if he was trying to kill me.

'I couldn't even manage to scream; and for the first time I saw his mother smiling. She was happy now!

'The wretch had made a real mess of me. I was bruises all over. But then, afterwards, when he came close, to kiss me, and to make love, I gave him such a kick in his stomach that he yelped like a castrated dog, and started to vomit.

'I'd had enough. At dead of night I went down into the stable, saddled up my horse, and off I went, off into the night, and I'd taken my husband's silver rifle with me.

'At dawn I stopped up on a mountain pass; down below, on the plain, I saw a dozen men on horseback, coming towards me. These were the men of my husband's family, coming after me.

'I took up my position, aimed the rifle, and fired. With the third bullet I hit one of the horses, and it crashed to the ground, taking its rider with it. I hadn't killed it, only wounded it. That stopped them. They did an about-turn, and off they went, as fast as they had come. As far as those bastards were concerned, their horses were worth more than a runaway wife.

'I returned to the town, and I went to work in a hospital, as a nursing assistant. To tell the truth, at the start I was more or less a cleaning woman. People who knew that I had run away from my husband looked at me as if I was a prostitute. They kept me on at the hospital, though, because it wasn't so easy to find women prepared to do the night shifts. Some of the patients actually refused to allow me to touch them. But even though they gave me a hard time of it, I enjoyed the work, and after only four years, I became head of the department.

'At the time of the Sinai war, and the Israeli victory, I wasn't in Palestine. I was in Egypt. I had been there for three years. My hospital had sent me to Alexandria, to do a special course in theatre nursing.

'I had been a communist for some time. Together with other Egyptian comrades, I was doing clandestine work. The official Communist Party in Egypt hadn't existed for many years; in fact, when Nasser came to power (thanks to the support of the working classes and the peasants), the first thing he did was to force the communists to dissolve their party. The Egyptian proletariat actually believed that the leaders of its party would hold firm, even if it meant going into clandestinity. But a large number of those leaders ended up joining Nasser's party. The rank and file of the party, and some of the leadership, didn't admit defeat, though. They continued their struggle, even though the party had been broken up. Nasser's police did a good job. They had spies everywhere, and every day they were arresting communists. I was arrested too, exactly two years after I arrived in Egypt. They locked me in the fortress prison in Alexandria. The one that stands on the canal leading into the port. One morning I woke up with a feeling of emotion almost bursting my heart: I could hear a band playing the *Internationale*.

'"What's that?" I shouted. "The revolution?"

'I stood up to look through my cell window.

'A big warship was sailing into the canal.

'There was a red flag on it.

'It was a Soviet ship.

'It was the ship which was bringing Brezhnev to meet with Nasser.

'There were many political prisoners in that prison. They began yelling and swearing and shouting abuse   . But the *Internationale*, played by Nasser's band, drowned them out. I couldn't stop crying. How could this be? There was Brezhnev, who was supposed to be a communist, hugging Nasser   and doing business with him . . . And there was me, a communist, locked up in one of Nasser's prisons.

'Then, after the Sinai defeat, and Nasser's crisis, there was a kind of amnesty. They set me free, and I went back home, or rather, close to my home, on the Jordanian side of the River Jordan.

'Later on I joined the Popular Democratic Front, where I had some friends. But it was not easy to stay in it. There were only about ten of us women, and the bourgeois elements were putting it around that we were riff-raff and prostitutes. And even the poor people had a low opinion of us. To the Arab way of thinking, a revolutionary woman is a cheap woman. But we paid no attention. We used to work in the tent towns, looking after the sick, and doing propaganda work.

'Then came the battle of Amman. We women were involved in the shooting too. Many other women followed our example, and came out into the streets. They picked up guns from the hands of the wounded, and began shooting.

'Then we had to leave. The leadership of the Front ordered us not to let ourselves be seen around in uniform any more. We went into clandestinity.

'They asked me if I was willing to join an armed action group which was intended to assassinate Mohammed Jaffis, one of Hussein's police captains, and a filthy torturer who had butchered dozens and dozens of our comrades. It was supposed to be an "exemplary" action. Because morale was low during this period, it would act as a sign that the underground struggle had begun.

'Already another woman, in Amman, had blown up a wing of a big American hotel, with two or three VIPs in it, and in Cairo a group of revolutionaries had assassinated Hussein's Minister of the Interior, Wasfi Tall, the man who had organised the repression in Jordan in July and September.

'Now it was Jaffis's turn.

'At the start I said that I was against revenge killings, but the Front's leadership convinced me that in a desperate situation like this such an example would give an important boost to the whole struggle.

'My task was to act as a bait for the captain, and to lure him to a house where a comrade would be waiting to kill him.

'I got myself hired as a private nurse for an old lady at the French Embassy, who was very ill. I remembered the blue veil of my mother's tribe, and I put it on, so that I could pose as a practising Muslim who went round veiled in the old style. Every day I passed in front of the building where the torturer-captain had his office. But every time he came out he always had an escort of two or three bodyguards. I felt like dying every time he came near me, but I soon succeeded in getting myself noticed. This captain dropped his guard one evening and accosted me as I passed. He passed a couple of rather heavy compliments my way, in a low voice. I stopped, and rounded on him, and started insulting him in Alexandrian dialect, like a street woman. At that point he began courting me for all he was worth. He used to come out and wait for me to pass in front of his house, but every step he made was watched by the men of the secret police, and they in turn were shadowed by our comrades.

'Finally the big day arrived. I agreed to meet him for a rendezvous at his place. One of our comrades was supposed to be in the flat, but it turned out that Hussein's police had got wind of something. Without saying anything to their captain, in order not to spoil his amorous adventure, they had stormed into the flat before we arrived, and had killed my comrade.

'The captain and I arrived just as they were carrying his body out. It was a terrible moment for me. I had to start play-acting, staring and crying, and carrying on as if I had no idea what it was all about. By the end, though, I was screaming like a hysteric, because it had finally sunk in that the policemen who had killed him were still there, in the other rooms, and they would be ready to kill me too at the first false move I made.

'I was trembling, but for real. I allowed him to console me and cuddle me and kiss me. I allowed him to make love to me. But first of all, I put up a big performance, to force him to get rid of the police in the other rooms. I started crying, and said that I couldn't make love if I thought that somebody else was there, spying on us. The captain was so eager to have me that he literally chased the policemen out of the flat.

'We made love. Or rather, he made love, and he wanted to carry on. He made the most of me, all night, and I had to wait until daybreak before I could kill him.

'I had brought a gun with me, which I hid in the bathroom. When daylight finally appeared, I got out of bed, as if I was going to the toilet. I went to the bathroom, and took my gun, and looked out into the garden. There was a policeman there, fast asleep on a bench. So I took a cushion, stuck the gun into the stuffing of the cushion, went over to the bed where the captain was sleeping, and shot him in the head. Without even a tremble, as if I was bringing him his morning coffee.

'Four shots. Four dull thuds, like someone banging on a wall. I looked out of the window into the garden, to see whether the policeman had heard. He was still fast asleep. I left the house, with no problems. I crossed the entire city on foot. Almost running. The police were all over the place. They were looking for a woman wearing a blue veil, in the style of a practising Muslim.

'A few days later they arrested two women. The newspapers denounced them as the two women who had murdered Jaffis. But in fact those two women had given themselves up voluntarily. And when the police interrogated them, it came out that they were lying. They beat them black and blue, and threw them out in the street. The chief of police referred to them as "the usual megalomaniacs". But then, within another few days, the police in Amman began receiving other letters from women who said that *they* had been the ones who had assassinated Jaffis. Within a month the desk of Hussein's chief of police was literally covered with hundreds of self-confessions. With this gesture the Arab women had found a way of expressing their solidarity with me; they wanted to show the whole country that, whatever the sacrifice, whatever the cost, they were with us, completely. With the revolution, with *our* revolution, the revolution of the Arab proletariat.'

translated by ED EMERY

The Bawd–The Christian Democrat Party in Chile

A drum kit stands centre stage: a bass drum with a pedal, a smaller drum, a snare drum, and various cymbals.
A number of singers with guitars stand at the back of the stage. They sing Chilean songs in low voices, as a backdrop for the words spoken by the actress.
A woman enters – or rather, a lady. She walks with difficulty, as if she has just been running hard. She is mumbling indistinctly and panting like a dog. She stops, and looks around, in desperation. She is crying. Before she begins speaking, the Chorus sing a verse of a Chilean song, in low voices.

I can't bear it. It's terrible, unbelievable   People being slaughtered, beaten to death   . (*She looks out over the audience, as if following the course of a long river*.) There, there . . a corpse .   two corpses .   floating .   . It's horrible! Stop it! Stop it! What are you doing? Brother against brother .   Killing each other   . Guns . Shooting .   (*She sits at the drum kit, picks up a drumstick and strikes one of the drums*.) Stop it! Enough of this killing .   ! Peace! Pray, pray for peace! Listen to your heart, listen to the voice of the Holy Father. (*She imitates the voice of the Pope. The Chorus sings, in the background*.) 'My Chilean brothers, I weep for you, for all of you .   . For those who have been killed, and for those who did the killing! For the officers, especially, because they, more than anyone, need the word of Christ's enlightenment!' (*The song begins again. She plays a military drum-roll, as if for a firing squad*.) But it was obvious, it was bound to end like this . .   This is where exaggerated rhetoric leads you. That president .   . I told him: (*She plays a drum break*.) 'You'd better go gently with some of these reforms!' (*She plays the drums in a slow rhythm, using brushes.*) What about the agrarian reform .   . Sure, that was in our programme too, the Christian Democrats' programme, but it's one thing to have a programme of reforms, and it's another to actually apply it! The true reformist doesn't put reforms into action; he just promises them. Otherwise he becomes a revolutionary! That was the big mistake of that lunatic Allende! But there you go, even his name was enough to tell you where the man was going: in Chilean, Allende means 'beyond'! That's right, beyond the bounds, beyond moderation, beyond reason, in other words, towards anarchy! It was bound to end up like this! Yes, of course, we were partly responsible too .   . We supported some of the expropriations, at the start, and even voted for them

   . But we were confused because of the situation .   . I repeat, this whole situation is crazy! Look at my fellow Christian Democrats in Italy: they voted through laws as much as twenty years ago, and they've *still* not put them into effect! That's what I call responsible government! But when people start deciding they're going to *do* things . . . positive action, new laws, changing things . . . Well, you can't expect to get away with upsetting the bourgeoisie! Some things have to be paid for . . . And who pays for them? The poor devils, the workers and peasants, who believed in it all, that's who.

At this point she speaks as if answering somebody's question.

'You mean who *you* deceived! (*She replies.*) Me . . ? Of course. It was my fault too! It's true. I supported the Allende government. Only thirty-six per cent of the votes for his Popular Unity government came from the Left. If I, the Christian Democrat party, had not supported them, they would never have come to power. When I asked Fanfani, Moro and Colombo, in Italy, they agreed with me supporting the Popular Unity front.

'Your boat is sinking,' they said. 'It's time to hand over the helm. For the moment!'

So we had to choose: either ally ourselves with the fascists, in order to make up a government, which would mean dirtying our hands and losing credibility . . . Or support the Left, and let the socialists and the communists run the country for a bit, so that *they* carry the can for the whole mess.

After a double drumbeat, she falls to the floor, dead. Then she picks herself up again, like a puppet come back to life.

That's a lie! Who said that? Yes, I know, people accuse us of manoeuvring so as to get the Americans to throttle the Chilean economy! They say that we moved heaven and earth to stop the international banks giving any more credits to our nationalised industries. Some bastard put round a rumour that our secretary, Frei, actually went to Rome to see Prime Minister Rumor, to ask him to block imports of industrial goods, and Fiat cars in particular, and that Agnelli blocked them immediately and completely? I even hear people saying that we organised strikes to paralyse the transport sector in Chile, and other sectors . . . dirty, mafioso tactics . .   When I hear these vile, shameful accusations, all I can say is . . 'Yes, it's true!' But what else could we do? The situation was becoming intolerable. The workers were going too far with the business of the nationalisation and socialisation of industry. I mean to say, for God's sake! There are industries and industries! There are those which *can* be nationalised. *Must* be nationalised, in fact, because they're non-productive and on the verge of bankruptcy – so you hand them over to the state, and get compensation at three times their real value. But there are also very profitable industries, belonging to individual American companies, and to high-ups in the Christian Democrat party . . . *us*, in other words . . and those mustn't be touched! These crazy workers . . . they were going off and expropriating left, right and centre, without even waiting for Parliament's say-so. And the same was happening with the peasants! They needed land? So they went out looking for uncultivated land, and, without so much as a by-your-leave, they set up cooperatives .

They'd simply take a red flag and stick it up in the middle of a field! They even took over a golf course and a hunting reserve! I ask you, can this be allowed? (*The song continues in the background.*) The government was in a dilemma: either it went along with the expropriations, or it would find itself with thousands, hundreds of thousands, of angry workers and peasants against it. There was an amazing consumption of bits of red cloth in this period! Vermilion, scarlet, carmine, cadmium, geranium, every kind of red . Linen, cotton, silk, artificial silk, nylon, you name it! They didn't bother with land deeds any more – all they needed was their red flags! (*She strikes one of the drums.*) As you went round the suburbs, every day there seemed to be a different factory with a red flag flying. I even saw a church in the slum area of Santiago with a red flag flying from the roof! You can't allow that sort of thing! They were going too far! And as we know, red attracts red . . And this time the red was blood! (*As she bangs her hand on the table, she knocks over a pot containing red paint.*) Because the military don't mess about when it comes to restoring order. As some general once said: 'What I call order is a tidy row of white crosses in a graveyard!'

And then the sale of black cloth began . . (*She notices the red paint on her fingers.*) Yards and yards of the stuff . . (*She tries to clean her hand with a rag.*) Whose stupid idea was it to put this paint on the table? I know. Somebody's trying to make a cheap point about the Christian Democracy having blood on its hands? Well, let me tell you, this is no time for jokes!

She rattles out the sound of machine-gun fire on the drums. The lights change with every rattle. The Chorus begin to sing quietly; a sad song. She changes character.

'My son . . . My husband . . Let me see them . . They're there, in the stadium, along with seven thousand others . I heard shooting last night . . . somebody told me that people were being executed! Let me see them   '

She resumes the character of the Christian Democrat party.

Don't you think that I suffer for these poor women . .
Suffer *with* them . . . ? Because I am them . . . ! I am the
people . . . We Christian Democrats are the heart of the
people! (*A beat on the drum.*) Ha, ha . That sounded
good, didn't it! Heavens . . . I was almost believing it
myself! Sure, it was a terrible massacre. But didn't I warn
Allende? 'Watch out, Allende, because things are going too
far!' Yes, of course, I did, and at the same time I was busy
digging his grave! And who's denying it?

And anyway, we know the story: if I hadn't given the word,
the military would never have moved!

Two nights before the coup, there was a vote taken at the
Christian Democrat party headquarters in Santiago. Result:
thirty-seven in favour of a coup d'état, ten abstentions, and
eleven against. Yes, it was *us* who decided on the coup. I
voted for it! I wanted it! You see how candid I am! You
don't really think that eighty thousand armed men would
have moved if they didn't have a political consensus behind
them, do you   ? And the support of an entire social
class, in other words, in our case, the upper and middle
bourgeoisie? (*A sharp drumbeat.*) What was that? A shot?
Have they started shooting again? (*Another sharp
drumbeat.*) Sounds like a shoot-out . . Oh no . . . it was
an execution . Just as well Single shots? Snipers.
How I hate those snipers! The last desperate fling of suicidal
terrorists . . They know their cause is hopeless . there's
only a few of them . they're poorly armed . . and
they're isolated!

At least, that's what our guerrilla warfare experts tell us
. . No, I don't mean guerrillas . . where are you going to
find guerrillas in our country? I'm talking about
theoreticians, researchers, specialists in urban guerrilla
warfare . . These researchers tell us that the Andes are
quite unsuitable for guerrilla warfare. They're too rugged.
Too cold, too, in the South . You'd freeze to death up
there. The central part of the Andes is more reasonable,

but it's only a small area, easily controllable by a well-equipped modern army like ours. What's more, sociological studies have shown that the peasant population of those provinces is not at all inclined to collaborate with rebels. They are a peaceful, submissive people. Simple, you might say.

The Chorus begins the song 'El Pueblo Unido.'

What was that bang? Eh? An explosion? Where? Casentas? Where is Casentas?! In the South?! The frozen South?! What's going on? A rebellion, you say? How many of them? Six . . . ? Six what . . . ? Six hundred . . . ? Six thousand!! Impossible! Technically impossible!! Six thousand people is the entire peasant population of the area! They're all peasants, you say? And they're armed . . . ? Who armed them? What do you mean, you don't know?! The carabinieri?! The peasants seized the barracks, and the guns were in the barracks?! The carabinieri's guns? So why do you give guns to carabinieri if they're going to let them be stolen?! (*A loud crash.*) But that sounds like artillery fire . . . (*Reassuring herself.*) Or maybe it was thunder . . (*She is frightened.*) A bomb? But where? In Santiago!! For God's sake! Now the soldiers are bound to get nervous, and react: tatatata . . . in the stadium! (*She is worried, and tearful.*) But what is the Holy Father doing . . . the Pope? 'My brothers . .' Is he going to recognise . . ? (*Relieved.*) The Pope has recognised the military government! Of course this fact will help save lives . . . We should forget politics and think of saving lives. Anyway, things are going well . . The Americans are supporting us, and funding us too . . And France, Britain and Germany . . . Everybody has recognised our military government. Italy not yet, for all that Piccoli and Fanfani are raring to go! (*A drum roll.*) Ah, if only something like this could be pulled off in Italy!

Listen how quiet and peaceful everything is! A deathly silence, you might say!

Everything is under control. The party's over. Order has

been restored. What's that mess of bodies there? Get rid of them at once. And fish out those bodies floating in the river.

The President of the United States has said that he's coming to visit us.

What's that you say – he's not coming? He says he doesn't want to compromise himself . . . He 'can't get involved with a coup d'état'? You really mean that not one single foreign head of state is coming to visit us? Not one? Not even the Italian Christian Democrats?

The Pope has promised, though .   The Pope says he's going to come.

Now the Americans are going to have to come out in the open.

They won't? In fact they're distancing themselves? They say that we're not good business for them. We've not been a good investment. They're fed up with lending us money.

The swine, they're cutting our funds!

We Christian Democrats have always said that it was dangerous to get involved with certain people. The military have never understood economics.

We're almost bankrupt. Batten down the hatches. Down with tyranny! Long live democracy! What we need here is a democratic patriotic front .   To oppose the military. Anyone who's in favour, come over here, under my petticoats. There's room enough for everyone!

No, not communists, though .   . I have my reputation to think of.

We want free elections .   . Down with tyranny!

What? The Pope is coming to embrace the tyrant? Oh God, what a gaffe . . . He must be crazy! He'll ruin everything for us! Down with the Pope!

Blackout.

translated by ED EMERY

Questions of Terrorism and Repression

Two monologues dedicated to Meinhoff and Moeller
I'm Ulrike – Screaming (1975)
It Happened Tomorrow (1977)
A Mother (1980)

Neither Franca Rame nor Dario Fo, they have made it clear, was ever in agreement with the murderous ideology which impelled the Baader-Meinhoff group – The Red Army Fraction – in Germany or with the Red Brigades in Italy; but Franca Rame subscribed to every word of Ulrike's scream of denunciation. What they have maintained is that the State must treat even its enemies as human beings with certain rights.

The first two monologues Franca Rame has described as 'obscenely tragic with the obscenity of our times'. Ulrike Meinhoff and Irmgard Moeller were both members of the Red Army Fraction, the German left-wing terrorist organisation. Ulrike Meinhoff was found dead in suspicious circumstances, which may have been suicide, in the maximum security prison of Stammheim in Munich. That was in 1976. In 1977 two other members of the Red Army Fraction, Andreas Baader and Gudrun Enslin, were found dead in their cells on the same day. Baader had shot himself in the back of the head – an almost impossible feat – while Enslin had hanged herself on a nail. The question was: who had pulled on her legs? Irmgard Moeller survived four stab wounds in the breast received in what was officially described as 'a suicide attempt'.

The third piece deals with the use of 'repentant' terrorists by the Italian state. Torture, physical and psychological, is often a catalyst of repentance and is embodied – even if invisibly – in the law giving special terms to 'penitents', which Franca Rame finds 'obscene'. It is a law which favours those members of terrorist bands who have most information to pass on to the authorities in return for reduced sentences. So the most brutal criminals have been granted pardons while minor figures have remained in prison. The 'supergrasses' have gone free.

STUART HOOD

I'm Ulrike – Screaming

Christian name: Ulrike.
Surname: Meinhoff.
Sex: Female.
Age: Forty-one.

Yes, I'm married.
Two children, born by Caesarean section.
Yes, separated from my husband.
Profession? Journalist.
Nationality? German.

I've been shut up in here for four years. Four years in this modern prison in this modern state.

Crime? Attack on private property and the laws protecting the aforementioned property. Attack on the consequent rights of the owners of property to appropriate ownership of everything beyond all reasonable limits.

Ownership of everything. Including our brains. Thoughts. Words. Actions. Feelings. Work. And love. In other words: our entire lives.

That is why you who control this state machine have decided to eliminate me .

We are indeed all equal under your sacred law. All, that is, except those of us who happen to disagree with you.

You have raised women to the dizziest heights of liberation. Heights? Yes, you have incarcerated me, a woman, in a men's prison.

Thank you.

You have rewarded me with the toughest of your prisons. Antiseptic. Glacial. Like a mortuary. And you subject me to the most criminal of all tortures: sensory deprivation.

What an elegant expression to describe what you've done to me: buried me in a sepulchre of silence. White silence. White cell. White walls. White fittings. Everything's white. Even the door. The table. The chair. The bed. Not to mention the lavatory.

The neon light is white. It's on all the time. Day and night. But which is day and which is night? How can I tell? Always the same light coming through the window. Fake. Artificial natural light. White light, as artificial as the window. As unreal as the time you've stolen from me. You've painted time white.

Silence. Silence from outside. Not a single sound. Not a noise. Not one voice. You can't hear anyone walking in the corridor. No doors opening or closing. Nothing.

Everything white and silent. Silence inside my skull. White as the ceiling. White like my voice if I try to speak. White, the saliva clotting in the corner of my mouth. White and silence in my eyes, in my stomach, in my belly swollen with emptiness.

I feel sick all the time.

My brain's coming away from my skull, bobbing in slow motion in the watery light of this room.

My whole body is like dusty specks of detergent churning around in this terrible washing machine called Stammheim. I'll collect them up, put the body together, put myself back together . I must resist. You *will not* succeed in driving me mad . . . I must think. Think! This is what I'm thinking: I'm thinking about YOU. You torturing me like this. I can see you, your noses squashed against the great glass walls of this aquarium you've got me floating in. You're watching me. Interested. You're waiting. Dissecting my living body. You're worried I might be able to resist. Worried others like me . . . your workers, perhaps, yes, your dependable lobotomised workers, you're worried they might suddenly wake up and try to spoil this beautiful world you've created for your own enjoyment.

How grotesque. You deprive *me* of all colour. Yet outside in that putrid grey world you've created, you're busy repainting everything in the wildest, most garish colours so no one will notice what it's really like. You force people to consume things dyed all the colours of the rainbow: coloured drinks, coloured food. Who cares if the dyes are poisonous, carcinogenic? So what?

You even paint your own women to look like demented clowns.

And you shut me up in all this white so that my brain shatters into fragments and smithereens, explodes like a bag of confetti. Sequins from your carnivals, your fun-fair chamber of horrors. Non-stop noise and racket in the streets, in factories, piped muzak everywhere! You probably even have it on in bed when you're making love. And you've shut me up in this aquarium just because I won't lead the life you lead. No, I don't want to be one of those women you manufacture and keep in cellophane wrapping. Frustrated! Exploited! A mother and a whore – both at the same time.

A slight rustle. The door's opening. It's the wardress with my meal. She's looking through me as though I wasn't here. As if I were transparent. She says nothing. She has 'orders' to say nothing. She puts the tray down and goes away.

Silence again.

Hamburger. Fruit juice. Cooked vegetables. An apple. Paper plate. Paper cup. No knife. No fork. Only a soft plastic spoon. It feels like rubber. They don't want me to take it into my head to kill myself.

When the right moment comes they'll see to all that themselves. And because there are no convenient bars on the window to tie a twisted sheet to – or a belt – so I can

hang myself – they'll give me a hand . . . or maybe more
than just a hand . . .

But I won't be the only one in this prison who commits
suicide. No doubt about that.
All the members of my group will have to die.

I know that for certain.
You've already decided that, haven't you, you up there in
the Government?

The slaughter will be carried out in a way that will make it
clear to everyone what we're dealing with: summary police
execution.

A state clean-up.
It will be a massacre intended as a warning to others!
To impatient young people, to protesting workers, to
insidious, non-conformist intellectuals. To discontented,
frustrated women.

The tale of how each one of us was found in our own cell,
hanged or dead from loss of blood or riddled with bullets.
That tale will be a manifesto nailed up for all eyes to see:

The eyes of immigrant workers . . . Turks, Arabs,
Spaniards, Greeks, Italians . . . A warning to beware of
going on strike . . . of marching in demonstrations,
protesting, provoking disorder!

Those who cause disorder are playing the terrorists' game.
Those who protest against the enforcement of unjust laws
are terrorists!

Those who protest and take to the streets shouting that
they're defending the quality of life . . . who scream for
clean air . . . for respect for the powerless – the old for a
start – thrown on the scrap heap like so much rubbish .
they're all terrorists!

Yes of course, we in the Baader-Meinhoff fell into a trap of
our own making. Perhaps the ideology of armed struggle
isolated us even from ourselves.

But beware 'Liberal Democrats', you are no better . . .
You're frozen solid with the fear they've sprayed all over
you from the aerosol marked 'Achtung Terroristen'. Every
movement frozen. Every thought frozen. Every impetus
towards decent behaviour.

The men who run this computerised system of ours have
trapped you in a state of constant panic: so that one small
mistake, a misunderstanding, a thoughtless piece of false
evidence and any one of you could end up like us:
swallowed by this great 'criminal-crusher' they call
Stammheim.

The state has uncovered the paralysing mirror of terror.
Our own corpses are reflected in that mirror. One look at
your own reflection and you're numbed; deep-frozen alive.

But those of you who accept these conditions, who have
darkness in your minds, who let your consciences fall
asleep, who look for a life without problems, a quiet life
    . I ask you: are you really sure you're still alive?

translated by GILLIAN HANNA

It Happened Tomorrow

They stabbed me in the heart. Four times. As if they
wanted to split it open. I couldn't scream at the first thrust
of the blade. All that came out of me was a noise, a rattle.
They threw something in my face that stunned me, maybe it
was ether, but I just managed to see them. There were
three of them, in military uniform. One of them grabbed
me from behind. By the hair. He twisted my right arm
behind my back, forcing me to sit down on the chair. The
other one held onto my left arm. He shoved a knee into my
groin, making me spread my legs apart, as if I was having a
back street abortion. The one holding my hair gave it a
yank so my head was wrenched backwards. I saw the blade
of the knife. One sharp thrust with the point of the blade
straight into the chest, almost on my left breast and then a
slash to the right and to the left. The blade was out. A gush
of blood soaking my stomach, my belly. Another thrust. A
pain, but sharper than the first time. This time I scream. As
the knife is wrenched out I feel the blade scraping against
the ribs under the breast – a kind of screech. Another gush
of blood, but not straight away. Then more, blood pouring
down, down, all over my belly. Down and down, drenching
me between the legs. My stomach's heaving. Something
coming out of my mouth. Maybe blood. Maybe just water. I
didn't feel the last two thrusts of the knife. I fainted for a
moment.

'That's it!' A dry voice woke me.

'Let her go!' I slid down, and out of the chair. I felt myself
falling, crashing onto the floor. My face pressed against the
tiles. The blood still gushing out. Pumping out with every

beat of my heart. My left arm is still folded under my
breasts. And I can feel the blood oozing out all over me.
Slowly. So slowly. It's trickling out onto the floor. I'm
paralysed. Whatever it was they threw in my face to make
me unconscious is working . . . or maybe I'm going . . .
'That's it!' . . . I say it too. 'That's it!' A few more minutes
and then it'll all be over. My eyes are wide open but I can't
move them. All I can see is a groove in the tiles filling up
with blood. Only out of one eye. The other eye is in
darkness, pressed against the floor. I feel instinctively – and
the feeling's getting stronger – that someone's watching me
through the spy-hole in the door. The same instinct tells me
to remain still. I try very slowly to move the fingers of my
left hand. It's hidden under my breast – just level with my
breast bone. Yes I can move the fingers. I've hardly
uncurled my fist when I realise my fingers are soaked by the
blood gushing out from between my ribs. I've found the
gaping edges of a wound. It's a huge gash. I go on probing.
I find the place where most of the blood is pouring from. I
squeeze it harder with my index and middle finger. The flow
of blood slows down. But there's still a lot coming from the
other wounds a bit higher up, under the breast. The spy-
hole is still open. I know because I can hear faint noises
from the corridor. Noise of hurrying footsteps. Noise of
locks clanging, doors slamming.

Shouts. Screams. Swearing. Shots.

'They're killing us all!' Enslin is in the cell next to mine. I
can hear her screaming. She sounds desperate. A voice
giving orders:

'Two loops in the rope. Two! Now pull! Both of you! Pull!
We'll hang her . . . Tie the rope up there.' 'Where up
there? The bloody thing won't hold. Keeps slipping.'

The one giving the orders swears.
'They made the walls in these fucking cells too fucking
smooth. Smooth as a fucking baby's bum. You'd have
thought there might be a pipe or something. Pass me that

box. We'll stick a nice hook up there. Yes that one. Go on, grab a hold of this hammer and bang it in.'

The sound of muffled hammering. Then more orders.
'Hold her steady. Hold her legs. Come on, lift her up. Put the rope through the hook. Come on. Now. Tie it off. Tie it. That's got it. Let go. Right. We're off. Next!'

'Hold on a minute. Untie her wrists first. Now get a move on. Out. Out!'

More footsteps. More keys jangling, locks clanging, shouts. Orders barked very loudly. Then a shot. Like a whiplash. The crash of a door being slammed.

Finally a voice passing my cell remarks:
'It's four. We can sound the alarm now.'

'No wait!' another voice cuts in.

'Let's give it another ten minutes. You can clear up. Clean everything up. Have a good look round before the judge and the doctor get here. Make sure there's nothing left lying about.'

'Open up this one. I want to have a look at Moeller, you never know.'

So here they are. My cell door opening again. The sounds, their voices, their words seem slowed down now – as if they're coming through cotton wool. Someone's speaking from the open doorway.

'Christ. This one's bled like a stuck pig. She's flooded the whole place out!'

'No, don't go in. You don't want to go wading around in that, do you? It's like walking in wet cement. You'd leave prints behind you.'

'OK. Well, there's no point in going in anyway. You can see she's bled dry.'

They close the door again. Footsteps. They re-open Enslin's door.

'Is she dead?'

'Yes, looks like it. What's this stuff? Look at this, here on the floor!'

A moment of silence. Then an order – screamed.
'Shut the door. Shut everything and get out. We've got to raise the alarm.'

A rush of footsteps. People running. Another silence. It lasts several minutes this time. There's no one left in the corridor. I try to move my hand. It won't. I can't do it any more. I feel a numbness spreading through my whole body, starting with my legs. I'm getting colder and colder as if I were being deep-frozen. The pain in my head is really getting terrible – a pain deep inside. I feel as if someone's stuck a knife into the nape of my neck. I can't breathe . . . I'm gasping .

I'm losing blood faster. The alarm is ringing in the corridor. Ten, twenty bells making a deafening row. I can hear people running – prison warders . . . they know where to go. They open the four cells . . . They hardly pause. Nothing said. A few minutes go by. Other people appear. Then stretchers. Two men come into my cell. I can hear them, but very distant. They pick me up. I can feel them swinging me. They feel my pulse.

'No I can't feel anything. The heart's punctured.'

'Yes this one's dead too.'

A priest has come in.

'Where are you taking her?'

'To the mortuary. All four of them to the mortuary.' They carry me past the cells of the comrades they've spared. The doors are shut. The doors are completely sound-proofed. They couldn't have known that anything was going on. And even if they did know; even if at this very moment they're screaming and throwing themselves against the doors, no one would be able to hear them. Complete silence everywhere.

I'm dying. I can hear the voice of the stretcher bearer saying:

'There's blood dripping all over the place. Hang on a minute. Let's bung it up with some wadding.'

I can feel them fumbling around in the wounds. They lift me up again. The trolley slides into the ambulance. I lose consciousness.

I wake up feeling my arm's on fire. Someone's stuck a needle into my wrist. He's squeezing a bag of plasma – that's the fastest way to get it into my veins. A nurse. Or maybe a young doctor. I've barely opened my eyes when he says:

'You were nearly a goner there. They thought you were dead. They were taking you to the mortuary. You'd lost so much blood your pulse wasn't beating any more. This is the second unit of plasma I've put into you. You would have bled to death on the marble slab if I hadn't noticed.'

I try to give him a smile of gratitude but I can't manage it. I look round. No men in uniform. I breathe a sigh of relief. At least I try. But something's stopping me. I feel as if there's a boulder weighing down my chest. They really thought I was dead. This young doctor has no idea what a mess he's dropped the police in with his last minute resurrection.

I manage a smile. But then I freeze.

'What if they get to me before I can talk. What if I never get to talk. Or what if I do. Young man – you have really messed things up. What a fiasco!'

translated by **GILLIAN HANNA**

A Mother

I . . . I don't just need your attention: most of all I need
your . . . imagination. Yes . . . imagine it. You are at
home, having supper with half an eye on the TV news. All
of a sudden a photo appears on the screen. A voice says:

'This is one of the terrorists caught after the killing.'
Christian name, surname. 'Ruthless criminal. Record of
violence.'

You stare at this passport-style photo . . . Jesus! It's
somebody you know. Your heart suddenly stops . . . stops
dead. My God! It's him! It's not possible, not possible.

It's not just somebody you know by chance . . . maybe one
of your neighbours' kids. No. No. It's . your own son.

It's *you* I'm talking to . . . Your own son. Impossible, you
say? Crazy? Why? You haven't got children? Well then,
your brother . . . or your sister. Imagine it. Just imagine.
Yes. Exactly. One of them . . her . . him . . a terrorist.

And it's not a mistake: he was caught with the gun in his
hand. He'd been shooting. He wounded a policeman,
seriously. Imagine it. Please, make the effort. Yes, I know
 . It's unbelievable. Your child, or your . . . your brother
. . . You know him, you talk to him every day, you know
his ideas. He's got a temper, but he wouldn't harm a fly.
He's against violence of any sort. *Against* it. He even
wanted . . to be a conscientious objector . . . he
wanted .

There you are: this is exactly what . . . what *I* used to think
every time I saw the face of one of those youngsters
arrested, in the papers or on TV. I used to tell myself:

'My child will never be one of them. Never!'

But that young man that you're looking at on your TV now, who looks like a decent enough person, that is my son.

Yes. That's my child. I . . . I made him. I gave birth to him. I fed him. No, no . . . not from the bottle, you must be joking! I breast-fed him. From my own teat. Because I thought: 'Supposing he grows up peculiar? What if he becomes a . . . a . . . deviant? It'll all be because of not breast-feeding him. Nipple deprivation.'

Then, while I was pregnant, I read some books. I . . . I learnt that a baby should play with its own poo. Otherwise it may grow up disturbed. Yes, yes, and with its pee too: it helps them to get rid of aggression. I let him do it. Laveuve recommends it as well, in one of his articles. 'Faecal period: let babies play with their own excrement. Let them taste it. Let them throw it at each other.'

In this way they'll get used to the shit that people will throw at them when they grow up!

I . . . I really gave my child everything: I breast-fed him, I cuddled him, I brushed my skin against his, I let him smash cups and glasses, just like the . . . the paediatrician said, so as to stop him ending up neurotic. I let him play with his poo for as long as he liked. But . . he has turned out violent.

He could have settled for joining a gang of hooligans: setting fire to buses, raping a girl or two . . . Just to let off steam. At least judges are understanding about things like that. But no: he's a terrorist. A terrorist.

I'm in torment. I can't figure it out. Where did it all start? When? I run back over our entire life, as if it was a movie. Over and over again. I run through from the beginning . But I can't . . can't find .

Today he . . . is 24. Ours is a democratic family: we've all been involved in politics at some stage. The lad grew up with . . . with our ideas. Student protest at school: everyone

was involved in it. In . . . in his room he had all the posters
of the big heroes of the moment: Mao Tse Tung, Che
Guevara, Ho Chi Minh. Vietnam . . . Vietnam . . . I
remember in particular one poster that you must all
remember seeing. A Vietnamese. A young Vietnamese girl
holding a sub-machine gun, standing in front of a gigantic
American pilot with his hands up. Goliath, toppled by a
young girl.

See? The impossible can happen, can't it! How very clear it
all was, then. So very simple. On one side were the goodies:
they were poor, but they had the right ideology: human
beings come first, along with generosity, equality and
freedom. On the other side were the baddies: bullies,
greedy, rich and corrupt. With them, their cars came first,
and . . . personal profit. They're evil. Evil always loses.
And 'good' always win!

I know: you're thinking what I'm thinking. Rhetoric.
Triumphalist populism. Yes, yes, looking back on it now it's
easy to pass comment, to say we went too far, we . . . got it
wrong. Obviously, all of you saw it coming, right from the
start: you knew that we were going to come a cropper. All
of you? Well, lucky you! Congratulations!

But I think I've got the right to a few . . . a few doubts.
Yes. For example, just a few days ago, in a public meeting,
I was listening to a well-known intellectual, an expert in
youth problems, one of those people who always know
everything, who always understand things way before
anybody else. He was passing judgement on '68, on the
stupid things done. And what a lot were done! He was
criticising the childishness, the triumphalism of '68: a lot of
little Lenins playing at revolution. Then, a few days later, I
happened to pick up a copy of an old newspaper. In it there
was a picture of him, him, our 'expert': he was wearing a
crash helmet, with a camouflage jacket and an iron bar in
his hand. One of the armed stewards defending the student
demonstrations at the State University in Milan. Part of the
servizio d'ordine. A 'Katanga'. Yes, that was their name,

wasn't it? Katangas. Now he's got himself a good job: he's in charge of cultural broadcasting on Channel 3: 'A Gourmet Chat'! Our 'Katanga' is now teaching us how to cook meatballs!

Speaking of the stewards, do you remember the demonstrations? The demonstrations . . . I wish I had a film projector here with me, so as . . . .so as to show you a film of one of the demonstrations of that period. Even the earlier ones, the ones organised by the Communist Party. Maybe the one organised by the dockers . . . the Genoa dockers . . . when the people were killed in Reggio Emilia. Just to look back, to remember what a lot of people were involved, how strong we were.

And what about the funerals. Do you remember the funerals? When one of our youngsters, young boys and girls, were murdered by the police, by the fascists. Burning anger, deep pain, unbearable tension, the coffin carried shoulder-high. Nobody felt ashamed . . . of crying . . . with clenched fists raised. And . . . our flags . . . our red flags . . . And . . . and . . . our slogans . . . You remember the slogans we used to shout? Did we shout them just to scare old ladies and shop keepers, or . . . were we fully aware of what . . . we were saying? If we shouted them nowadays . . . we'd be put in prison. You were there as well, weren't you? Or maybe not . . . maybe it was just me and my son, disturbing the peace and disrupting the public order?

Anyway, look, I'm quite serious. I'm going to switch on a projector and show you some of the pictures from a demonstration which ended in a pitched battle right here . . . here . . . in our town. You might recognise some . . . familiar faces. And . . . and you might even see your own!

No, don't worry. Don't worry: I'm only joking. I couldn't pull a stunt like that on you. All of a sudden, a judge would appear from nowhere – Calogero-style. He'd grab all the pictures, he'd immediately start investigations, and he'd issue a hundred or two hundred arrest warrants. And I'd be billed as the usual Bulgarian spy. Relax . . . Relax.

I wish you could go through what I'm going through now. Wracking my brain, trying to understand where, when and how it all began. Because, you see, at home we used to talk with the boy. We used to talk, and discuss. Obviously, we didn't always see eye to eye: sometimes we'd have big arguments. Sometimes it all ended up in ugly scenes. It must have happened to you, I'm sure. For instance, one night he came home with a friend. He asked:

'Mum, can Aldo, [that was the boy's name] stay for a few nights?'

'Of course he can: your friends are always welcome. Yes, of course.'

But then you start to wonder. Hasn't he got a family of his own? I asked:

'What's the matter? Did you have a row with your folks?'

He was embarrassed . . . a bit evasive . . . but then the real truth came out: this Aldo was scared that an arrest warrant was about to be issued against him.

'The police have arrested some of the comrades from his organisation. But he left the group ages ago. He's got absolutely nothing to do with it now. I promise you, Mum, he's definitely innocent.'

So I said:

'But I don't understand. You, young man, if you are absolutely innocent, what are you afraid of? You just go to see a lawyer, he takes you to see a judge, and you tell him the truth.'

At that point my son burst out laughing as if I had just told him the funniest story he'd ever heard.

'But where do you think you're living, Mum? I can almost see it in the papers: "Young man, twenty-four, gives himself up to a judge. The judge is moved to tears, gives him a kiss and sends him off to a remote high-security jail".'

'Look, son: I really think you are over-generalising. There
are plenty of very honest and correct judges around.'

My son couldn't stand it any longer – probably because I
then said something so stupid that I can hardly still believe
that I said it. I said:

'Obviously, if the young man has something to hide, or
something a little bit shady, then I can see why he comes to
hide here.'

'The real reason, Mum, [and he said it really angrily] the
real reason is that you have joined the Party of the People
With Clean Hands. The Pontius Pilates of this wonderful
society of people who are dead from the neck up. Rule
no. 1: be suspicious of everything and everybody. Don't get
involved. Play it safe. Civil rights. "Be careful, son, they'll
take you for a sympathiser". This shit government has got
inside your heads and created a psychosis against . . .
against plague-carriers. Yes. We're like plague-carriers. In
the Middle Ages, when someone died of plague, their
friends, relatives and acquaintances were walled up in the
same room with them.'

Then, at this point, he calmed down and added, in a
controlled voice:

'For the short time I still have to live on this planet, I don't
want to join the sleeping masses. I want to do something, at
any cost.'

Just like that. 'At any cost'. At the time, I didn't attach any
importance to this 'at any cost'. In fact I hardly noticed it.
But now, of course, in the light of what's happened, it's
obvious that this 'at any cost' had a very precise meaning.
One of those . . fashionable, 'common-sense' style
psychologists, an Alberoni kind of person, with his big Ugo
Foscolo whiskers, would probably comment:

'Madam, your son was possessed by fear of darkness. He
solved his personal insecurities about not being anyone by
throwing himself into violent, spectacular action.'

It's easy for him, the ratbag, it's easy. I . . . I feel awful. I
feel as if I were a letterbox into which people drop
postcards, messages of all kinds. I watch the television . . . I
read the papers, I listen to people . . . the few who are still
willing to talk to me. And they all try to convince me that
some kind of horrible cancer has lodged in my son's brain.
That this idea of the armed struggle sprouted
spontaneously, like a poisonous fungus. All of its own
accord, eh? Without anybody, anybody giving a hand.
Without anybody pushing him a bit. Little by little, the fool
sprouted wings and turned into the Angel of Vengeance.
Bit by bit. Then he threw himself into exacting justice for
the powerless, sleeping, stupid masses. All on his own.

No . . . I . . . with respect. Without arrogance, I humbly
ask you to respect my intelligence. How could he have done
it all on his own? How can it be that nobody – I say not one
of us, of you, of them – feels that they have even the
slightest responsibility for what has happened?

Should we blame it on reading the wrong books, eh?
Misreadings of Lenin? And what about the show-trials?
They last ages, and they serve to divert attention from the
hundreds of Fascist killings, such as Brescia, Bologna, the
Italicus train bombing, Milan . . Didn't they have an
effect?

Injustice, I say. Injustice! All over the place: scandals,
unbridled corruption; thousands of workers thrown out of
work; people without houses; thousands of youngsters
alienated and criminalised.

That's enough! Stop it, please. Stop annoying me. What is
this? A rally? How long do you intend carrying on with this
sermon? Things are rotten – we're well aware of that. But
you're not going to claim that any of these things had an
effect .   ? YES!! They *did* have an effect.

I'm sorry. I apologise for making you embarrassed. I can
almost guess . . . what you're thinking. 'Poor dear, she's
beside herself: she is a mother, after all. Poor woman – with

her son in such a mess, you can't expect reasoned political arguments from her. Let her get if off her chest, poor dear.'

No, listen . . . . I'm really not interested in that 'poor dear' stuff. Let's take another example: another lad, a friend of my son's, a comrade who grew up with him, a pillar of strength. He was involved in politics in a practical sense. An extraordinary lad. He was a militant in the Young Communist Federation. Now he's a drug addict. Heavy drugs. Can you explain what went wrong with him? Misunderstanding Lenin in his case too? He's shooting two grams of heroin per day.

He had almost finished his degree course in Engineering Sciences. He was already working in his dad's firm. But then he went haywire. And when he has withdrawal symptoms, in order to stop him going out mugging, dealing drugs, burgling, killing, his father gets into the car and – himself – goes looking for the stuff. He's in touch with all the dealers in the area. All of them. Then, two months ago, the police got him. The father, I mean. They arrested him and charged him with dealing in and possession of narcotics. This wonderful new law!! And nobody in the family could care less: not the son, of course, but not even the father. Nor his wife. A little while ago, that family would have preferred to have their throats cut rather than lose respectability. Now they don't care. They're just two miserable people enslaved by their junkie son.

Before I discovered that my son was a terrorist, I used to think: 'If I was in their shoes, I would lock him indoors and chain him up. Yes, I'd chain him to a chair and smash his head with a hammer'. No way would I go out buying the stuff for him! It's all their fault. They've been too soft with him. Molly-coddled him.

A few days ago, I met that . . . that woman. We talked about our experience and our pain. At a certain point she comes out with this: 'I envy you, because at least your son believes in something. Mine cares only about needles and shooting-up'.

'What are you talking about? What you are saying is horrible. My son believes in a crazy utopia. My son shoots people, he's a killer. Your son isn't hurting anyone apart from himself.'

'Do you really think so? Look at the two of us: do I and my husband still look like human beings? Are we alive? Certainly, nobody will ever arrest my son for having done away with us. Look at the two of us: we're ghosts. If I could go back to when I was pregnant, I would have an abortion. Damn him!'

She said that 'damn him' with such feeling that my flesh still creeps to think of it.

'I feel the same way. If I thought I was going to have another child, I would strangle him. I promise you. It's all the fault of those bastards who made up the motherhood myth.'

I went to the prison in Sardinia, to visit my son.

I had such anger within me. I thought: he'll not get a single tear from me. Not one. I will tell him: 'This is exactly what you deserve, you fanatic. Are you satisfied now?' No. I won't tell him even that. No emotional display, no pity, because I went . . . I went to see the corpse of one of those young policemen murdered by my son's comrades. Yes, I went to the funeral parlour. Because it's too easy to complain about things if you don't see them at first-hand.

I arrived at the prison, a high-security prison. It was frightening even from the outside, let alone inside. I had a couple of cases with food and clothes in them. I turned up at the window they told me to go to. The officer told me:

'Sorry, ma'am: nothing's allowed in. According to regulations, Article 90.'

'Well, but . . . I've only brought some food. Everything is properly sealed, as per Prison Regulations.'

'Sorry. Article 90.'

'All right then . . .'

I went and sat in a corner. The other relatives were not giving up as easily as that: some of them shouted and yelled and got angry. One woman in particular was shouting at a policeman during the argument:

'Don't call my son a terrorist. My son is a Communist Fighter!'

I was afraid for her. Then they turned another woman away. They sent her away, and I didn't understand why. Her son was there, and she had her visiting order. They . . . they refused to let her in. She had to go all the way back to her small village, up by Reggio Emilia.

Another four relatives were turned away as well because the people they were visiting had been transferred to another prison, but . . . nobody would tell them which one. I was lucky. I had a visiting order; my son was there and . they let me go in.

First of all I went into a little room. There was a woman in charge of searches. She said:

'Get undressed.'

I didn't understand. I said:

'But . . . what do you mean, "get undressed"?'

'Get undressed completely, madam. For the vaginal and anal search.'

'You must be joking. Why on earth should I do something so . . . so disgusting? What right do you have to ask me? I've already been searched with the metal detector. I've got absolutely nothing on me apart from this dress and my handbag. I will be talking to my son through glass. This is just plain harassment, personal violence.'

'Prison regulations, Article 90. If you want to go in, get undressed; otherwise you can go home.'

I see. That's it, I suppose. Imagine it . . . you must imagine it. I felt I was being treated like . . . like an animal. I got undressed, but all the while I was thinking:

'All right, then, I will get undressed. But I'm telling you, you'll regret it, I promise you. As soon as I get out of here I'll report it. I'll write to the papers. Oh yes I will.'

But then I just felt like laughing: write to the papers? But what newspaper is going to publish anything on what I am going through now? I . . . I am only the mother of a terrorist. 65% of people in Italy are in favour of capital punishment . . . I . . . I opened my legs and let her get on with the job.

'Remove your hairpin, your necklace, your watch, lock your handbag, cigarettes, and everything else in here. Here you are: take the key. This way, please.'

I went in: long corridors, iron bars, gates, keys. I've never seen so much iron all in one place.

Finally I entered a . . . , a huge hall, divided down the middle by a sheet of glass from floor to ceiling. A very thick glass. And every four feet of this glass was divided by an iron bar, to define your space. On the other side of the glass were the prisoners. On this side, men, women, relatives were shouting their heads off to make themselves heard. There was no internal phone, no microphone, nothing. The din was like being in a crowded railway station.

'Where is my son? Excuse me. Where . . . ?'

I see him almost immediately. He's over there, behind that sheet of glass. I go over. Here he is. I look at him, again and again. I recognise him . . . not from his face, which is swollen and bruised, but from his jumper . . . He kept his hands in his pockets . . . He never took his hands out of his pockets. I only . . . understood why later . . . he'd had them broken during a transfer. Not because of a riot, not at all. They'd been taken in a van and beaten up. Or rather, they'd been beaten up and then taken in a van. How many . . . how many years will he get? twenty? thirty? Isn't that

sufficient punishment? Why all this . . . this glass . . . all
these beatings? Why not kill them on the spot, as soon as
they catch them? Just shoot them in the head.

Oh no, of course, that can't be done. Sorry. I keep on
forgetting that we live in a democratic country . . . in
theory. The Germans are so much better at these things.
There the terrorists are just killed outright, at Stammheim.

I look at my boy through the glass. My child. You know,
the first time I saw him, when he had just been born, I
watched him through glass then too, the glass of the aseptic
room at the hospital. I don't know if you find the same: my
boy has grown up, has become a man, but I still see him as
a child. Even when I dream of him, that is the way I see
him. I always dream of him when he was little.

A few nights ago I dreamed about him being brought to
trial: he came into the court escorted by two carabinieri.
One on either side, holding him. He looked like about five
years old . . . no more than that.

When he saw me, he tried to . . . to smile. Then he burst
into tears. The judge said to me:

'Please, madam, would you pick him up and make him stop
crying. Otherwise I'll have to suspend the proceedings. I
have to question him.'

They sat me in the witness box, in front of a microphone.

'You have to cooperate, madam.'

'I beg your pardon? In what sense do I have to cooperate,
your honour?'

'In the sense that you have to convince your son to
collaborate. We shall take his youth into consideration. He
must tell us everything he knows: names, surnames,
addresses. In other words, he has to repent. He has to
inform.'

'My son a repenter, an informer?'

'Precisely, madam. Think of Fioroni, of Sandalo. They committed unspeakable crimes, but once they decided to cooperate with the authorities, we freed them. Now they are happy, rich and abroad.'

'But your honour, my son joined the Red Brigades only recently. You said so yourself. This was his first action.'

'Yes. But unfortunately this will not be to your boy's advantage. This new law on supergrasses is an advantage only to those who personally organised the armed squads, those who enrolled the members and armed them, who pointed out which legs, which heads to shoot at. Think of Savasta, madam: what a marvellous case. He murdered seventeen people and informed on 240. That's a repenter in the real sense. In a couple of years he'll be free. Yes, obviously we sentence people like him to years of imprisonment, but in two years' time he'll be out. When he enters the courtroom to witness – likewise with Barboni, Peci and Viscardi – the carabinieri stand to attention. Even we magistrates stand up as a sign of respect. Soon they'll be playing the national anthem for them!'

'Anyway, let's get back to your . . . get back to your lad here. Let's see if we can help him a bit. Here we have a list of names: he has to indicate which ones he knows. If he hasn't met them in person, it doesn't matter. Even if he's only heard of them, that'll do. Finally, if he's not really sure about them, it doesn't really matter either, because we shall arrest them, and then we'll see what comes out at the trial.'

'But your honour, what do you mean: "we'll see what comes out at the trial"? That way you run the risk of involving innocent people; you run the risk of a blow-up.'

In my dream, as I said the world 'blow-up', it was just as if I'd said a magic word. From underneath the judge's bench, smoke started pouring out. I got frightened.

'What is it? A bomb attack?'

'No. Keep calm. It's just steam from the radiator valves.'

The carabinieri jumped on me.

'Madam, your son's no longer on your lap. Where is your son? You were responsible for him; you were in charge of the defendant-child. Where have you hidden your child?'

'Wait a minute. I haven't done anything. I'll look for him.'

I drop to my knees, under the smoke. I find my child. Here he is. I've caught him.

'Your honour, here he is. Oh my God! No, this can't be my son. This is the drug addict boy. His body is covered with burns, he's bleeding. What happened? What happened?'

'They have tortured me. They've burned me all over, my testicles as well. I've got the names of five policemen. I'm going to report them.'

'Silence! Shut up. Shut up! Your honour, here's my boy. I caught him, I'm handing him over to you. I've done my duty as a responsible citizen who trusts our democratic institutions. Here you are, sir . . . Oh, I'm sorry, your honour. I've held him too tight. I've strangled him. He's dead.'

translated by ED EMERY